NATHAN READ:

HIS INVENTION OF THE MULTI-TUBULAR BOILER AND PORTABLE HIGH-PRESSURE ENGINE, AND DISCOVERY OF THE TRUE MODE OF APPLYING STEAM-POWER TO NAV- IGATION AND RAILWAYS.

A CONTRIBUTION TO THE EARLY HISTORY OF THE STEAMBOAT AND LOCOMOTIVE ENGINE.

BY HIS FRIEND AND NEPHEW

DAVID READ.

NEW YORK:
PUBLISHED BY HURD AND HOUGHTON.
Cambridge: Riverside Press.
1870.

RIVERSIDE, CAMBRIDGE:
PRINTED BY H. O. HOUGHTON AND COMPANY.

PREFACE.

The successful application of steam-power to boats and locomotives forms a most important era in the history of this world's progress; and the men who took a part in accomplishing that great work, are entitled to the remembrance of all such as respect human genius, and look upon the advance of knowledge and civilization as a blessing. The subject of this memoir was one of those men, and the interesting incidents relating to his inventions were liable to be lost to history by the lapse of time, and with them his just claims for the essential part he took both in the invention of the steamboat and locomotive engine. To preserve these facts, was indeed the motive that led to the preparation of this little volume.

The facts relating to the inventions of Nathan Read, so far as they were spread on paper, were preserved by him during his lifetime, and by his family after his decease; and the reasons why they were not published by himself, will appear in the closing chapter of this book. He having, however, failed to accomplish this end, which is much to be regretted, the question arose, should the evidence of his labors pass off forever, or be presented to the public?

This was a matter that upon every consideration both of a private and public character scarcely allowed hesitation; the truth of history, the dictates of friendship and justice, and the claims of Science to a knowledge of all who have been devoted to her service, seemed to require the publication; and under this aspect of the case the labor of collecting the evidence and preparing it for the press was undertaken by the subscriber, without expectation of fee or reward. And it may be added, that a desire to contribute to the early history of the steamboat and locomotive this additional testimony of the talent and genius of our own native citizens, will also, it is believed, be appreciated by a generous public.

In prosecuting our inquiries we have found it necessary to compare the respective claims of inventors; but this occupies no distinct portion of the narrative, and is drawn from the facts here presented, and from the published accounts of various authors; and such extracts as have been deemed proper to elucidate the subject, or to give interest to the reader, have been duly credited, by reference to the authorities.

It will be seen that different projectors, supported by different countries, come in as contestants for the honor of these inventions: England, Scotland, France, and Spain, claim the invention of the steamboat; and France and England the locomotive engine; when, in truth, they were both inventions of our own country; and it will be left for the reader to decide who among us contributed most toward the invention of that machinery, which resulted in their success.

The original descriptions, plans, and drawings of Judge Read, so far as they relate to the subject, have been carefully copied into this volume; and, on inspection, no one will doubt the genuineness of the papers. His manuscripts, in the mean time, contain numerous plans, drawings, and descriptions, of other inventions and experiments in the mechanic arts, made by him. These, and many other matters, would properly come within the scope of a biography, but not within the plan of this work.

To show the necessity of a complete revolution in the steam-engine to prepare it for navigation, even after Watt had made his great improvements upon it, a brief account of its invention as it progressed from one step to another, from its earliest history up to the close of Watt's improvements, has been given. The engine of Savary, Newcomen, or Watt, could not be successfully applied to boats; and all attempts made with them utterly failed; which in itself shows the fallacy of all the claims to the invention of the steamboat, before the discovery and existence of machinery necessary to give it success. In order to show this, it became important to notice the numerous experiments, both in this country and Europe, with the old form of engine, whether of Newcomen or Watt, or those tried by Rumsey and Fitch; and, to show wherein their failure consisted, to compare their engines with that afterwards invented by Read, which it is claimed was the engine applied by Fulton on his first boat upon the Hudson, and led to the final success of navigation by steam.

The same may be said of the numerous experiments with the locomotive engine. All proved unsatisfactory or wholly failed until the multi-tubular boiler and high-pressure engine, which had been invented by Read to fit Watt's engine to the purposes of locomotion, gave triumphant success to the locomotive, as applied by George Stevenson.

These various inquiries make up an interesting portion of the volume; and although they may be felt at first to be inapplicable to its general purpose, yet, as the reader progresses, he will see both the necessity and importance of this portion of the narrative; more especially as the design of the work is purely historical.

DAVID READ.

BURLINGTON, VT., *October*, 1860.

CONTENTS.

CHAPTER I.

CHAPTER II.

CHAPTER III.

CHAPTER XIII.

CHAPTER XIV.

CHAPTER XV.

ILLUSTRATIONS.

NATHAN READ AND THE STEAM-ENGINE.

CHAPTER I.

The invention of the steam-engine prepared the way for a series of experiments, with a view to apply it to navigation, and at length to land transport. The great improvements of Watt had changed its character from a machine of comparatively small importance, and limited in its application and use to the single purpose of pumping water and lifting ore from the mines, to an instrument applicable to the use of mills and factories, and most kinds of mechanical industry, where a stationary motive power was required. This essential change in the utility of the steam-engine, was effected, not only by reducing the expense of working it, but by converting the rectilinear motion of the old Newcomen engine into a rotary motion, uniform and continuous; which improvement not only made it *possible*, but a convenient motive power, to turn the wheels of mills and factories.

It is very proper here to notice, that the invention of the steam-engine, which in its operative power at this day far exceeds the whole amount of hand labor upon the habitable globe,[1] was not the work of one man, or one generation of men; indeed, we may well imagine

[1] *London Quarterly Review*, vol. civ. p. 411, 1858.

that the force of steam must have been known to some extent, as early as man had the power of observation and fire and water were brought in contact before him. From the time Hero of Alexandria amused himself by the use of steam as a mechanical force to move the simple machinery he had invented, up to the time Watt perfected his improvements and set his double-acting rotary-engine at work, was nearly two thousand years. And although no sensible improvement was made with steam force, before Cardan discovered the effect of condensation, — for the æolipile used by the Greeks and Romans, and Jack of Hilton, of feudal notoriety, were no improvement upon Hero's invention, — yet from Cardan's day to the time of Watt, a period of some two hundred and ten years, scientific men and men of genius were successively engaged in the work, and adding something towards the invention of the steam-engine. Battista della Porta, Solomen De Caus, the Marquis of Worcester, Torricelli, Pascal, De Garricke, Papin, Savary, Newcomen, and others, not forgetting little Humphrey Potter, each one made some important addition to it. Notwithstanding this, when it went into the hands of Watt it was at best but a very imperfect thing, compared with engines of the present day. To suppose that the steam-engine, steamboat, or locomotive, could be invented by one man, would be contrary to the truth of history. Indeed, inventions in steam-power, and in most cases of like complication and importance, have been progressive. It would be absurd to suppose, that one single mind would be able to acquire, in the first place, so perfect a knowledge of all those intricate principles of natural and mechanical science, as it must needs understand, to construct a steam-engine; and in the second place, conceive and put together the several parts of a machine so complex and extensive. Facts show that these inventions are brought about by successive improvements, first by one and then by another. How often do we hear the remark, "Fulton invented the steamboat," as if everything connected with it, keelson, hulk, wheels, and the engine it carries, were new discoveries by him alone.

Indeed, to Watt himself, who never had any settled purpose or intention of applying steam power to boats or land carriages,[1] and made no special improvements in the engine directed to those purposes, there is due a large item of credit, in both cases, for his inventions. The steam-engine, however, as improved by him, was but partially prepared for navigation and land transport. He gave it the rotary principle,[2] without which it would have been useless; but his massive boilers, and great weight of fuel and machinery, were not suited to the capacity of boats and land carriages, nor was the form of his engines adapted to those purposes. His double-acting cylinder and separate condenser, would both apply to boats; but in the case of land carriages it became necessary to dispense with the condenser, the working beam, and some other parts of the machinery, for the want of water for condensation, as well as the want of space; and a new sort of engine, constructed upon different principles, became necessary for that particular use.[3]

It is believed that Nathan Read, as early as 1788–89,

[1] Muirhead's *Life of Watt*, p. 330. [2] *Ibid.* p. 227.

[3] Woolhouse *On the Steam-engine*, vol. i. p. 42.

while a resident of Salem, Massachusetts, invented the necessary machinery to adapt Watt's engine to boats and land carriages, with the avowed and special purpose of applying it to both of those objects. That he constructed a model of a steamboat, with paddle-wheels and his improved engine to drive it, being the same machinery, substantially, that Fulton used eighteen years after, in his first experiment upon the Hudson; and being also the first combination of that machinery which gave Fulton his success, and success to the application of steam-power to navigation. That he at the same time constructed a model of a land carriage, to run on common roads (and equally applicable to a railroad-track), and fitted his engine, with special reference to that purpose, upon the high-pressure principle, dispensing with the condenser and working-beam; which machinery was substantially upon the principle as that which gave Stevenson his success, and which is now in use for locomotive engines.

The evidence relating to these inventions of Read is mainly derived from the papers he left behind him at his decease, the originals of which are open to the inspection of any who may have the curiosity to examine them, from which the extracts and drawings contained in this publication have been taken. It is proposed to examine this evidence, and compare it with the claims of other projectors.

CHAPTER II.

NATHAN READ [1] was a native of Warren (formerly Western), Worcester County, Mass., born July 2, 1759. His ancestors originally came from Newcastle-upon-Tyne; they then settled in the County of Kent, where they lived for several generations. From thence they emigrated to America at an early day, about 1632, and settled in the vicinity of Boston, where they resided for many years. His grandfather — when the country was new, and but few settlements in that section of the State — purchased a large tract of land in Warren, upon which he settled, and where he spent the remainder of his life in the improvement of his lands. His father, Major Reuben Read, was an officer in the Revolutionary service; and his mother, whose maiden name was Tamison Eastman, was first cousin to Major-General Nathaniel Greene, of Rhode Island. His father was an only son, and resided upon the homestead during his life. At the age of fifteen years, Nathan commenced his preparatory studies for College, and at the close of the summer vacation of 1777, entered Harvard University. His parents were desirous that he should qualify himself for the ministry, and he

[1] The likeness of Judge Read faces the title-page. It was engraved at Philadelphia during his attendance there as a member of the House of Representatives in Congress, in 1801–2, at which time, he was in the forty-second or third year of his age. The likeness is a very perfect one, and is struck from the original plate, which has been preserved in the family.

attended Professor Sewall's Lectures on the Hebrew Language. He acquired a good knowledge of the language, and by appointment, gave a Hebrew Oration at a public exhibition of the University; and during the interval between the death of Professor Sewall and the appointment of his successor, Mr. Parsons, he was engaged to instruct the class in Hebrew. He graduated in 1781, on which occasion he was selected to deliver the valedictory address. He was distinguished as a scholar, and left College with the respect of officers and students. After graduating he was engaged in teaching in Beverly and Salem, until 1783, at which time he was elected a Tutor in Harvard University, where he continued his labors as such until the commencement of 1787. He then resigned his place as Tutor, and entered upon the study of medicine with Dr. Edward A. Holyoke of Salem, until October, 1788, when he gave up the idea of following medicine as a profession, relinquished its study, and opened an apothecary store in Salem.

While engaged in the study of medicine with Dr. Holyoke, and also while in his store, he devoted himself, more or less, to study and experiment in the mechanic arts, which indeed held a higher place in his mind than his medical studies or merchandise. It was during this period of time that he invented and constructed his models of a steamboat and locomotive carriage, before noticed.

In October, 1790, he was married to Miss Elizabeth Jeffrey, daughter of William Jeffrey, Esq., Clerk of the County of Essex, and granddaughter of Joseph Bowdish—August 24th, 1791, he was elected a member of the American Academy of Arts and Sciences — April 4th, 1795, he removed to his farm in Danvers, and built a permanent structure across Water's River, which served the double purpose of a dam and bridge. In 1796, he and his associates erected and put in operation the Salem Iron Factory, for the manufacture of chain-cables, anchors, and other materials of iron, for ship-building, he having the chief superintendence of the work. While thus engaged, he invented and put in operation in the factory, designed for its own special use and benefit, with a view to the saving of labor and other economical purposes, a nail machine, since extensively used for cutting and heading nails at one operation, for which he received a patent, as the original inventor, from the United States Government, on the 8th of January, A. D. 1798. This highly important invention obviated the very great labor and expense of the manufacture of those articles by hand.[1]

In October 1800, he was appointed a member of Congress for Essex South District, to fill the vacancy occasioned by the death of Judge Sewall, then late member from that district; and in November 1800, he was elected by the people of the district, a member of the succeeding Congress, for two years from and after March 4th, 1801; and was a member during the severe contest in the House of Representatives for the Presidency, between Jefferson and Burr.

In February 1802, while a resident of Danvers, he was appointed by Governor Strong a special Justice of the Court of Common Pleas for the County of Essex; and after his removal from Danvers to Belfast in

[1] For his specification and patent of the Nail Machine, see Appendix, No. 1.

Maine, which was in 1807, he presided as Chief Justice of the Court in Hancock County for many successive years. In 1815, he was elected an honorary member of the Linnæan Society of New England.

After removing to Belfast, Judge Read gave most of his time to agricultural pursuits; but he often indulged himself in new inventions in the mechanic arts and trying experiments therein; and during his whole life these and the natural sciences were his favorite study. He invented several useful agricultural implements, for some of which he took a patent; but constructed them mainly because he had use for them on his farm. His farm consisted of some four hundred acres of land, finely situated near the head of Belfast Bay, lying upon the shore just south of the City of Belfast. His residence overlooked the bay, with its attractive scenery; and here he spent the remainder of his life, ever taking a lively interest in all matters of a public character, especially such as were designed to improve the moral condition, and advance the intellectual and social improvement of the people among whom he lived. He regarded the cause of education as involving one of his highest duties; and at an early day, when the town was comparatively new, he was instrumental in establishing a high school in Belfast, that the youth of the place might be educated at home — the beneficial effects of which have long been appreciated.

He died at his residence in Belfast, January 20th, 1849, in the ninetieth year of his age, and in the full possession of his intellectual powers, except a few days at the close of his last sickness. He possessed a strong constitution, and a strong and highly cultivated mind; his aims were high, and he soared above the sordid interests of the world. He never sought to make himself conspicuous, or to give publicity to his attainments or labors, but chose rather unobtrusive retirement. His deportment was always gentlemanly; his form fine, and his countenance highly intellectual. His conversation was ever interesting and instructive; and he lived and died with the respect and esteem of all who knew him. He was the last surviving member of his College class; and with two exceptions, — Judge Farrar and James Lovell, — the oldest living graduate of Harvard University.

As early as 1788, as already noticed, while a resident of Salem, he became especially interested in the purpose of applying steam-power to the practical end of propelling boats and land carriages. He foresaw the importance of attaining such a purpose, and set himself to work to contrive the necessary machinery to effect it, which at that time was felt by all intelligent men who had given their attention to the subject, to be a *desideratum*, — a work yet to be accomplished. The idea as applied to boats was not new; various experiments had been tried, but were mainly directed to the mode of propulsion, without so much attention to the motive power; and all the experiments hitherto tried had proved a failure. To show the nature of those experiments, I will briefly notice them in their order, that the reader may judge of the cause of their failure, and of the necessity that then existed of great improvements in the steam-engine, in order to make the application of steam-power to boats and land carriages successful.

CHAPTER III.

It has been seen that Watt's double-acting condensing engine, containing the continuous rotary principle, was not introduced to public use in a working form until 1787, which principle, though not so designed by Watt, was one of the necessary prerequisites to a successful application of steam-power to navigation. Hence the inference is beyond dispute, that success in the invention of the steamboat before that time had not been effected. Indeed it will appear, that whatever had been done, both in speculation and experiment, proved that there was no lack of the idea, or want of faith, in navigating boats by steam; but the faith was without the appropriate works.

The earliest pretension we have on the subject of steam navigation, has been dug up from the national archives at Simancas in Spain, and purports to be a paper discovered in the year 1825, long after steam navigation went into effect both in America and Europe.

The following is a translation [1] of the account, from "Navarrete's Coleccion de los Viages," etc., Madrid, 1825: [2] —

"Señor Don Thomas Gonzales has sent me from Simancas the following notice: —

[1] Credit is due to the Hon. George P. Marsh for the original account, and the translation of it.

[2] Vol. i. p. cxxvii.

"'Blasco de Garay, a sea-captain, proposed to the Emperor and King, Charles V., in the year 1543, an engine to move vessels and large ships, even in a calm, without oars or sails.

"'In spite of the obstacles and opposition which the project met, the Emperor ordered trial to be made, and this in fact took place in the port of Barcelona, on the 17th of June in the year 1543.

"'Garay never publicly exhibited his machinery, but at the time of the trial, it was observed that it consisted of a large caldron of boiling water, and wheels of propulsion attached to the two sides of the ship.

"'The experiment was tried with a vessel of 200 tons — which had lately arrived from Colibre with a cargo of wheat, — called *The Trinity*, and commanded by Captain Pedro de Scarza.

"'As commissioners on the part of Charles V. and the Prince Philip, his son, there were present on this occasion, Don Henry of Toledo, the governor, Don Pedro Cardona, the treasurer Ránago, the vice-chancellor, the master accountant of Catalonia, D. Francisco Gralla, and several other persons of condition both Castilians and Catalans, and among them several sea-captains, who were present at the experiment, some on board, others on the beach.

"'In the report made to the Emperor and the Prince, they all agreed in praising the machinery, and particularly the facility of steerage of the ship. The treasurer Ránago, who was unfriendly to the project, states that the vessel would make but two leagues in three hours; that the machinery was complicated and expensive, and that there was much danger of the frequent bursting of the caldron. The other commissioners declared, that the vessel would put about twice as quick as a galley by ordinary navigation, and that she made at least a league an hour.

"'The experiment being concluded, Garay took out the engine which he had set up in the vessel, and having deposited the wood-work of it in the arsenal at Barcelona, kept the rest in his own possession.

"'Notwithstanding the objections raised by Ránago, the plan of Garay was approved, and if the expedition in which Charles was then engaged had not prevented it, he would no doubt have encouraged its prosecution. However he promoted the inventor one grade, gave him a compensation of 200,000 maravedis, ordered all his expenses to be paid out of the general treasury, and conferred other favors upon him.

"'All this appears from the original records and proceedings deposited in the royal archives of Simancas, among the state papers belonging to the affairs of Catalonia, and of the department of war, both military and naval, for the year 1543. "'THOMAS GONZALES.

"SIMANCAS, 17*th of August*, 1825."

Mr. Marsh adds the following note to his translation: —

"BURLINGTON, *March* 26, 1860.

"DEAR SIR, — The above is the translation I mentioned. Navarrete is a man of very high authority. He may have been imposed upon, but as Gonzales must have been officially connected with the office of the archives, it seems improbable that he would have fabricated the story, though it looks a little incredible upon the face of it.

"Yours truly,

"GEORGE P. MARSH.

"Hon. D. READ."

It would not be regarded as proper to treat the above account as a fabrication without further information on the subject. It purports to be a matter of public record, and is detailed by Navarrete (who is reputed to be a faithful historian), no doubt as he received it from Gonzales. Under those circumstances the account must be taken as true, unless there is good reason to suppose that it found its way into the archives as a hoax, or what would be more likely, as a fraudulent mode of attaching to Spain the credit of inventing both the steam-engine and the steamboat. As we trace the connected history of the invention of the steam-engine, it is, however, extremely difficult to arrive at any conclusion favorable to the authenticity of the account.

The experiment of De Garay is stated to have been made in 1543. This was one hundred and fifty years before the steam-engine was so far invented as to be applied to any working purpose, and two hundred and forty years before Watt made it capable of turning a crank, and long before we have any reliable history that steam was ever thought of as a motive power. In 1543, and from that time back to Hero of Alexandria, who lived some one hundred and thirty years before the Christian era, and who was the first to notice the expansive force of steam, of whom we have any account,[1] it had never been applied to any mechanical use of moment. Hero, to gratify his curiosity and love of science, conducted steam from an iron pot into a small hollow ball or sphere, with two pipes passing out of it at opposite sides and bent at the ends in opposite directions, through which the steam would escape, and by its reacting force, give to the ball

[1] Stuart's *Anecdotes of the Steam-engine.*

a rapid rotary motion, to the delight of the inventor. (See figures Nos. 1 and 2.) These simple toys, with another more simple still, called the æolipile,[1] or ball of Æolus, used by the Greeks and Romans, — and we have one account of its being used by the Normans in Staffordshire after the Norman Conquest,[2] — constituted all there was of the steam-engine, not only at the time, but for a long time after the reputed experiment of De Garay at Barcelona.

The æolipile consisted of a hollow ball of the size of a common pot, made of cast-iron, with a small open pipe connected with the top, and passing off in a horizontal direction. (See No. 3.) By filling the ball partly with water and placing it over a fire, the steam, as it was forced through the pipe, produced a lateral current of air, and thus served for the bellows of that day, for blowing up flame and producing combustion,[3] like the blacksmith's bellows of the present day. It being a windy little instrument, was named after Æolus, the god of the winds. The æolipile referred to in Staffordshire, was somewhat different in its construction, and used for a different purpose. It was connected with one of the old feudal customs of England, and was called *Jack of Hilton*. For the amusement of the reader I will give the description of it as related in Plot's "History of Staffordshire." [4]

"Yet there are many old customs in use within memory,

[1] Vitruvius, lib. i. chap. vi.

[2] Plot's *History of Staffordshire*, p. 433.

[3] Renwick *On the Steam-engine*, p. 202.

[4] *Natural History of Staffordshire*, by Robert Plot, LL. D., p. 433. Oxford edition, A. D. 1686.

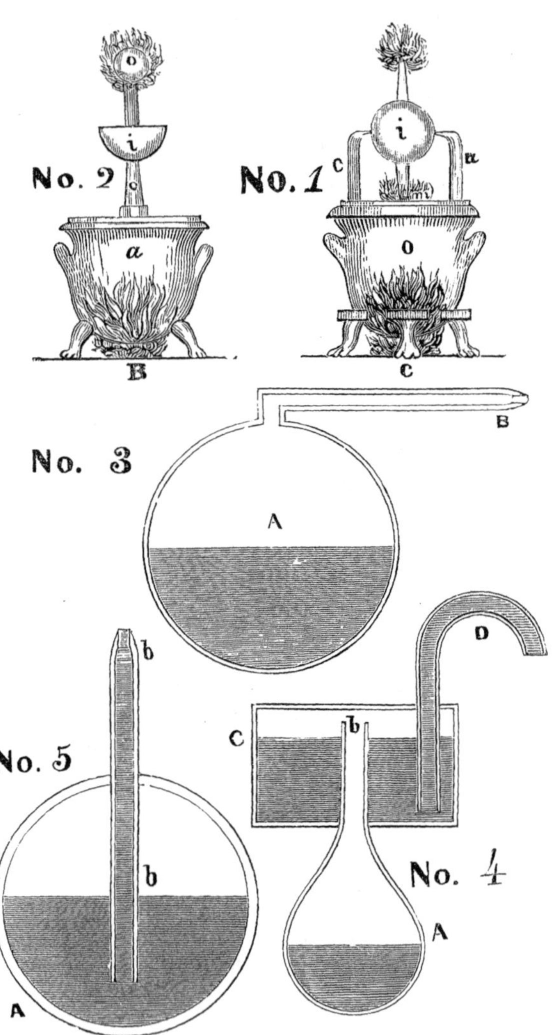

No. 2
o
i
a
B
No. 1
i
c
a
m
o
c
No. 3
A
B
No. 5
b
b
A
D
C
b
No. 4
A

of whose originals I could find no tolerable account, that possibly might commence as high as these times: such as the service due from the Lord of Essington in this county (Stafford) to the Lord of Hilton, about a mile distant, namely, that the Lord of the Manor of Essington shall bring a goose every New Year's Day, and drive it round the fire in the hall at Hilton, at least three times (which he is bound to do as mean lord), whilst Jack of Hilton is blowing the fire. Now, Jack of Hilton is a hollow little image of brass, of about twelve inches high, kneeling upon his left knee, and holding his right hand upon his head, ... having a little hole in the place of the mouth about the bigness of a great pin's head, and another on the back about two thirds of an inch in diameter, at which last hole it is filled with water, it holding about four pints and a quarter, which, when set to a strong fire, evaporates after the same manner as in an æolipile, and vents itself at the smaller hole at the mouth in a constant blast, blowing the fire so strongly that it is very audible, and makes a sensible impression in that part of the fire where the blast lights."

With these two simple things, representing all there was of the steam-engine at that day, had De Garay suddenly brought one into existence, of sufficient magnitude and power to propel a ship of two hundred tons burden about the Bay of Barcelona, it would seem that an achievement so wonderful before the world would have had some historical mention of it aside from the record which for the first time came to light in 1825. Moreover, with what propriety can we suppose that any single mind, "in the year 1543," a mere twelvemonth, at a period too when the dark ages still cast their shadows over the intellect of man, and the arts and sciences were but little known, was capable of grasping the invention, both of the steam-engine and steamboat, and that without any previous invention of the kind to lead the thought to such a conception, or rule or formula, to give direction, in the construction of its complicated machinery?

As we look forward from the reputed experiment of De Garay we are still more struck with the difficulties that come in the way of credit and belief in the account. Cardan was the first modern author who makes any allusion to the subject of steam.[1] He seems to have had some knowledge of its expansive force; and in the course of some experiments in chemistry he was making he discovered that steam might be condensed and a vacuum thus produced. He gave an account of his experiments in 1576, in a work he then published, — being some thirty-three years after De Garay's reputed experiment. This was the first known step, after Hero's invention of the æolipile, that led to the invention of the steam-engine, and it was an important step.

Battista Porta published a work in 1601, in which he gives some account of experiments made by him in steam; wherein he showed the effects of condensation, and the vacuum thereby produced, by forcing up water to fill the vacuum by atmospheric pressure. He also invented a machine for raising water by the expansive force of steam alone; causing it to press downward upon the surface of the water in a cistern,

1 Renwick *On the Steam-engine*, p. 203; Stuart's *Anecdotes of the Steam-engine*, p. 19.

and thus force it up through a pipe passing down into the water;[1] and he in the mean time, determined the relative bulk of steam and water.[2] His experiments both in mechanism and chemistry, effected another important step in the invention of the steam-engine.

Solomen de Caus, about forty years after Porta, was the next to make any experiments in steam. In 1641, he constructed a machine to raise water by means of a boiler and pipe, and the downward pressure of steam upon the surface of the water.[3] His machine was similar in principle and construction to Porta's, and it does not appear that he made any very great improvements upon it. He sought the patronage of the French government to aid him in his steam projects; and to get rid of his importunities, it is related of him that they declared him a crazy man, and confined him in the Bicètre, the insane hospital at Paris. This was near a hundred years after the reputed experiment of De Garay under the very eyes of the French nation.

About twenty years after De Caus, the Marquis of Worcester constructed a steam-engine, worked by the expansive force of steam, and set it to pumping up water in Vauxhall Garden in London.[4] This was the first working experiment, ever tried by steam, above the æolipile, and has given to the Marquis of Worcester the reputation of being the first who invented the steam-engine. It was rude in its con-

[1] See No. 4. [2] Renwick *On the Steam-engine*, p. 204.

[3] See No. 5. Muirhead's *Life of Watt*, p. 91.

[4] Stuart's *Anecdotes of the Steam-engine*, vol. i. 1829.

struction, and not put to any steady use, but only to show by experiment that steam might be made to fling water into the air some thirty or forty feet, to the astonishment of the London public; and in 1663, — one hundred and twenty years after De Garay's account,— he obtained an act of Parliament for his "Water-commanding Engine."[1] Afterwards, when the steam-engine became so far improved as to make it a valuable motive power, English and French writers entered into a controversy upon the subject, the former claiming the Marquis of Worcester, and the latter De Caus, as the inventor of the steam-engine — each class of writers prompted by national pride. They seemed to have no knowledge of De Garay's experiment, as no allusion was made by them to the subject.

During the very time the Marquis of Worcester was trying his experiments, and following thereafter, a school of illustrious men in Europe were engaged in scientific study and experiment. Galileo, who was by the Inquisition and the rack forced to renounce those truths in natural science which he had discovered, conceived the true nature of a vacuum, and communicated his ideas to his pupil Torricelli; who, after the death of Galileo carried out the suggestion by a series of experiments, in which he succeeded in producing a more perfect vacuum,[2] and in the mean time invented the barometer. De Guericke[3] meanwhile invented the air-pump, and also the cylinder and piston; he exhausted his cylinder with the air-

1 Muirhead's *Life of Watt*, p. 93.

2 *Ibid.* p. 101; *Cyclopædia of Biography*, p. 312.

3 *De Arte Mechanicâ Hydraulicopneumaticâ*, 1657.

pump, and established the principle of atmospheric pressure by means of the piston. Pascal determined the weight of the atmosphere by its pressure upon the piston, and the variation in its weight at different altitudes.[1] Boyle also invented an air-pump, and assisted Torricelli in making his experiments at Florence. They together constructed a machine to raise weights by atmospheric pressure alone, which was the origin of the atmospheric engine.[2] But it does not appear that any of these distinguished men attempted to produce a vacuum by condensation, which idea all this time rested with the suggestions of Cardan and the experiments of Porta. Yet the discoveries they severally made were not only necessary, but furnished important steps in the invention of the steam-engine.

The danger of explosion from the expansive force of steam, during these experiments had been discovered; and Denys Papin,[3] in 1688, to remedy the difficulty, invented the safety-valve, one step more in the invention of the steam-engine. He also attempted to produce a vacuum by rarefying the air in the cylinder by heat, then to raise the piston by the explosive force of gunpowder. These failing, he built a fire under the cylinder, which he partly filled with water, and found the steam would lift the piston to the top, and by removing the fire, as the steam cooled, the piston would fall. But the idea of applying and removing his fire from under the cylinder, every time he gave an upward and downward motion to the

1 Nouvelli's *Expériences touchant le Vinde.*

2 Muirhead's *Life of Watt*, p. 101.

3 *Arta Eruditorum*, 1683 and 1690.

piston, presented a practical difficulty that discouraged him; and he gave up the subject for the time being.

Some ten or twelve years after, Savary [1] happened to think that Papin's difficulty might be overcome by having a boiler separate from the cylinder, and by applying cold water outside the cylinder to cool the steam within it more rapidly. This worked better, but gave no practical importance to the engine as a working power, but plainly disclosed the fact that its utility depended on some contrivance to produce a sudden condensation, which would give to the piston a motion upward and downward equally sudden. Savary, however, did not succeed in effecting this grand purpose; but his experiments were highly important in the progress of the invention, for which he obtained a patent by act of Parliament, in 1698; [2] and drawings were made of his engine — being the first known time the steam-engine was represented on paper.

The next advance in the progress of this invention was made by Newcomen and Cawley, in 1705. They inclosed the cylinder with another of larger size, with a space between of eight or ten inches for cold water for condensation — an improvement upon Savary's plan of affusing cold water on the surface; — they also applied leather packing to tighten the piston, and covered the top of it with water resting upon it for the same purpose, and improved the engine by attaching eduction-pipes, valves, cocks, and a variety of small

1 *Phil. Trans. Abr.* vol. iv. 198, A. D. 1699.

2 Woolhouse *On the Steam-engine*, pp. 5, 6, 7.

and ingenious work, to give the machinery a more perfect action. They also invented the working-beam, and by a mere accident[1] discovered the process of injecting cold water into the cylinder for condensation, without which the condensing engine must have remained comparatively useless. Noticing that the piston moved with more rapidity and force than usual, they searched for the cause, and discovered a hole through the piston where a plug had worked out and let the cold water into the cylinder. A sudden condensation of the steam and more rapid motion of the piston was the result. This opened to their minds the idea of injecting cold water into the cylinder — which plan was thereupon adopted. They invented and applied for that purpose the injection-pipe, with its ingenious apparatus, through which a jet of water was flung directly into the cylinder, and the steam almost instantaneously condensed. This gave a corresponding movement to the piston, and the steam-engine, for the first time, if I am allowed the expression, had the breath of life breathed into it and became a living soul.

This invention made way for another, equally curious and of much importance. The injection-pipe and apparatus above mentioned, were controlled by two valves, the one opening and the other closing alternately, and controlling the action of the engine. These valves were worked by hand brakes, and being easily done, they usually employed a boy to tend them. A lad of the name of Humphrey Potter,[2] getting tired

1 Deragulier's *Ex. Phil.*, vol. ii. p. 533.

2 Muirhead's *Life of Watt*, p. 119. Renwick *On the Steam-engine*, p. 220.

of his work, took it into his head to attach the brakes or handles that worked the valves to the working beam, and leave them to be moved by its alternating motion, while he could rest his weary self and enjoy his play. This incident resulted in the invention of the scoggin (and afterwards the governor), which not only gave a more regular and uniform motion to the piston, but increased its upward and downward movements from about eight to sixteen times in a minute, thus doubling the effective power of the engine. It thus became, with the exception of fire to feed it, a self-governing machine, settling at once upon that degree of motion which the most free injection of steam, and sudden condensation, could give to it.

It was now thought that the steam-engine was perfected; and the young Hercules, though rough and clumsy in its workmanship, and awkward in its movements, was, for the first time, of which we have any knowledge, set to work in good earnest pumping water and raising ore from the mines.

The engine of Newcomen, however, was far from being perfect, either in the principles of its construction, or in its workmanship. It was yet incapable of propelling a boat or locomotive engine, yet it labored away in the mines and nowhere else, for the next eighty years, without any essential improvement.[1] Smeaton, however, improved the finish and proportions of the machinery and constructed an engine, from which he made a table of proportions for the use and benefit of mechanics engaged in their construction.[2] It may be

[1] Muirhead's *Life of Watt*, chap. xix.

[2] Smeaton's *Reports*, vol. i. p. 223, and vol. ii. p. 338.

well to observe that the engine of Newcomen was moved by atmospheric pressure alone, and steam was used for no other purpose than as a means of producing a vacuum, not even to force up the piston, which was raised by a counterpoise or weight; it is hence called the atmospheric engine. Such was the condition of the steam-engine, when it came into the hands of Watt, its great improver.

The first step taken by Watt[1] was directed to a more economical use of steam, and to that end he entered upon a series of experiments to determine whether the estimated densities of steam and water were correct. He found that water when changed into steam expanded from seventeen to eighteen hundred times its bulk; and on this calculation ascertained that six times as much steam as was necessary was used at each movement of the piston. He invented the condenser, a vessel separate and distinct from the cylinder, to remedy this great waste of steam. The steam was conducted into the condenser before it was cooled, and he thus kept the cylinder hot; at the same time he closed the upper end of the cylinder, and added another induction-pipe, making one above as well as below the piston, by which the steam was alternately let into the cylinder, as the piston rose and fell; and substituted steam force, instead of atmospheric pressure, for forcing the piston down, and in lieu of the weight for forcing it up. These improvements gave twice the power at less than half the cost of the Newcomen engine. In 1769 a working-engine was constructed after this plan.

1 Muirhead's *Life of Watt*, recently published, we regard as the best authority in relation to Watt's improvements.

Soon after this, Watt entered into copartnership with Mr. Boulton of Birmingham, and the distinguished firm of Boulton and Watt was thereupon established.

Boulton was a man of fortune, and liberal withal, and Watt now had every facility to give free play to his inventive powers; and he handled the steam-engine as a half-finished thing. He readily saw, if it could be so constructed as to be used in mills and factories as well as in the mines, it would vastly extend its usefulness and increase its demand. This could only be done by giving it a continuous rotary motion, and thus enabling it to turn a shaft or wheel with uniformity, and to overcome the dead points of the piston, or momentary state of rest at each end of the cylinder, in reversing its movements.

To accomplish this desirable end, he constructed an engine with two cylinders instead of one; and applied his steam force to two cranks on the same shaft set at an angle of one hundred and twenty degrees from each other, with a fly-wheel and weight on the periphery of the wheel, at an angle of one hundred and twenty degrees from each crank. But since the above invention of the double engine, it has been found that the double-acting cylinder, and single crank, with the fly-wheel, are all that are requisite to give this motion.

He also invented the parallel motion, by which the angular motion of the piston-rod, hitherto worked by a rack and chain attached to the end of the working beam, was changed to a direct rectilineal motion. This was looked upon by other engineers as a curious "mechanical puzzle," and Watt himself said, "that he was more proud of his parallel motion than of any other invention he ever made."[1]

He also invented the throttle-valve, by which, from the action of the engine itself, the same amount of steam always entered the cylinder, and gave a steady, uniform motion to the spindles used in the manufacture of cotton and other fibrous substances; and to regulate those valves without personal attention, he invented that elegant and ingenious part of the steam-engine, the governor, by which the steam is cut off from the cylinder as the engine increases in motion, or is let in as it decreases, until their action and the action of the engine are balanced. He also invented the counter, gauge, and indicator, all useful in their place.

It was a slow process to construct the first engine, after these inventions were completed, embracing as it did these new, curious, and complex additions to its machinery, without any rules, plans, or drafts for them, other than such as lay in Watt's own head,—his marvelous, unrivaled, inventive brain,—and they were four years constructing the first engine designed for sale. This was completed in 1786, and put at work in the Albion Mills in 1787. Thus Watt, who, to use the words of Sir James Mackintosh, "stood at the head of all inventors in all ages and nations," by one invention after another at length succeeded in completing his double-acting rotary condensing engine, but far, even yet from being fitted for propelling boats or land carriages.

I have thus gone through with a concise account of the invention of the steam-engine, from the experi-

[1] Muirhead's *Life of Watt*, p. 242.

ments of Hero to the time Watt completed his improvements, for the purpose of showing how difficult it would have been for De Garay or any one individual to have conceived this whole invention, and so far perfected it in the short time of five or six months (as the account shows) as to have brought it to a practical working condition, for any purpose; much more to have applied it also in the same space of time to the propulsion of a vessel of the size spoken of in De Garay's experiment.

In addition to the above it is proper here to notice, that the account of De Garay presents the only instance in which Spain pretends to have taken any part either in the invention of the steam-engine or steamboat. After the reputed experiment of De Garay, and during that period of time when these inventions were in progress, embracing some two hundred and sixty years, and while France, Italy, Germany, Great Britain, and the United States were all more or less engaged in the work, and making their contributions to it, Spain, for aught that appears, was wholly insensible to the subject. This surely does not look as though she had at a former day interested herself in the matter: if so, her genius had departed.[1]

[1] Since the above was written, I have been informed that the paper referred to, purporting to be found in the archives at Simancas, has been proved a forgery. — AUTHOR.

CHAPTER IV.

As we proceed with the invention of the steamboat, we find that the thought of applying steam to navigation was entertained by nearly all the principal projectors of the steam-engine. De Caus,[1] the Marquis of Worcester, Sir Samuel Morland, Papin, Savary, Newcomen, Watt, and others, entertained the idea that it might be so applied, but no one of these individuals ever made the attempt to try it. Paddle-wheels had occasionally been used from an early period to propel boats by animal power, even by the Egyptians, and afterwards by the Greeks and Romans; and the latter in one of the Punic wars are said to have transported their troops to Sicily on boats with wheels turned by oxen. Valturius in his "Science of War," published in 1472, speaks of this mode of transportation. They were also mentioned by William Bourne in 1578.[2] And Prince Rupert, after retiring from his military life, turned his attention to scientific pursuits, and about 1680, constructed a boat upon the Thames, propelled by paddle-wheels, which were moved by horses,[3] and others used them in like way. So it is quite evident that the use of wheels of some sort, moved by

1 See De Caus' Book, *Les Raisons des Forces Mouvantes*, etc. Paris, 1615.

2 Muirhead's *Life of Watt*, p. 330.

3 Papin's account from *Acta Eruditorum*, Leipsic, for 1690, pp. 410–414.

animals to propel boats, was an old matter, but the application of steam-power to paddle-wheels was of more recent origin.

It is claimed in England, "that one Jon. Hulls,[1] on the 21st of December, 1736 (the same year Watt was born), obtained a patent from Parliament for what may strictly be considered a steamboat." Hull's theory — for it appears he never tried any experiment — was certainly a very ingenious one.[2] He published a pamphlet which he entitled, "A Description and Draught of a new invented Machine for carrying Vessels and Ships out of or into any Harbour, Port, or River, against Wind and Tide, or in a Calm." He made a drawing of his proposed boat, from which it appears that he intended to use one paddle-wheel in the centre of the stern of the boat, to be turned by means of ropes and pulleys, so arranged as to give his wheel a continuous rotary motion.[3] The plan of his boat has but little resemblance to a steamboat; and his machinery would lack the two essential qualities of strength and durability. He intended it only for towing other vessels out of or into harbors, and designed to move it by the Newcomen engine, the only engine then in use, and that so imperfect as to be in no way adequate to the

[1] Woolhouse *On the Steam-engine*, vol. i. p. 14. Woodcroft's *History of Early Steam Navigation.*

[2] Hulls' engine: Let *a*, *b*, *c*, be three wheels on one axis, and *d*, *e*, two wheels bore on another axis. *A* with ratchets so as to move the axis only when they move forward; *f*, *g*, *h*, are three ropes, and *P* is the piston of the engine. When the piston descends, the wheels *a*, *b*, *c*, move forward, and the ropes *g*, *h*, cause the wheels *c*, *d*, to move the wheel *e* forward and the wheel *d* backwards, and the latter raises the weight *G*, which moves the wheel *d* forward during the ascent of the piston; consequently the axis *A*, *B*, with the paddle-wheel, would be constantly moved round in the same direction and be an equable force. (See No. 6.)

[3] See plan, in Woolhouse *On the Steam-engine*, p. 15.

purpose designed. It is evident Hulls never built a boat or tried to put his theory into practice; had such been the case, English writers, in their zeal to prove him the inventor of the steamboat, would not have failed to mention it. His plan was no doubt found impracticable and abandoned; yet it showed that not only the idea of applying steam to boats was entertained by Hulls, but that he drew a plan on paper, of such machinery as he had invented for that purpose. Belidor, an eminent writer and engineer, who gave an account of the steam-engine in 1739, two years after Hulls published his pamphlet, makes no mention of him.[1]

In 1753, sixteen years after Hulls published his pamphlet, Daniel Bornouilli, who sought to propel boats by ejecting water from the stern, gained a prize from the French Academy of Sciences, for demonstrating to the Academy the point that steam-power, as then understood, could not be successfully applied to navigation, without a continuous rotary motion,[2] which it did not possess. This looks as though Hulls' rotary mechanism could not have been regarded of much if any importance. This, however, was not the only difficulty, the enormous amount of fuel required to run the Newcomen engine for any length of time, was beyond the capacity of a boat to hold or carry. Yet others, not seeing these fatal difficulties in their way, still persisted in trying their experiments with it.

Genevois, in 1759, tried a boat with the Newcomen engine and paddles, constructed after the fashion of a

[1] *Arch. Hydr.*, tom ii. pp. 300, 331.
[2] Renwick *On the Steam-engine*, p. 279.

duck's foot, opening in its backward and closing in its forward motion through the water.[1] But he soon found that art would not construct from inert lifeless matter, a paddle that would work with the elasticity of the living sinews, joints, and filaments constructed by nature. The Comte de Auxiron in 1774, and the Earl of Stanhope afterwards, made similar trials, but with no better success.[2] Perrier in 1775, it is said, tried paddle-wheels, but he could not make engine and wheels go together, and ascribed his failure of success to the wheels, which he flung aside, and tried other modes of propulsion, but discovered no plan of success.[3] The Marquis de Jouffroy, in 1782, constructed a boat at Lyons, one hundred and forty feet long, fifteen feet beam, and drawing three and a half feet of water; and launched it upon the Soane, where he experimented with it for more than a year.[4] He used paddles, which together with the defects in the prime mover, could not be made to work to his satisfaction; and the boat, after a long and thorough trial, was given up. But Jouffroy was entitled to great credit for his energetic experiments, and failed because the right sort of engine and propelling machinery were wanting.

The next experiment in Europe, worthy of notice, was tried by Patrick Miller of Dalswinton in Scotland, in 1787.[5] He put three small boats or skiffs together, side by side, making a triple boat, and placed paddle-wheels between them, to be turned by cranks, worked by men. This craft was built for a little pleas-

1 Renwick *On the Steam-engine*, p. 279. 2 *Ibid.* 3 *Ibid.*

4 *Dictionnaire de Physique*, Art. "Chaloupe a Vapeur."

5 Woodcroft's *History of Early Steam Navigation.*

ure boat upon Loch Dalswinton, a small lake upon his estate. It was moved about the lake with safety, but its slow movements were somewhat monotonous. One James Taylor suggested to Miller the idea of putting a steam-engine into the boat, and in 1788, he employed William Symington to construct a small engine for that purpose, which he put into the boat in the autumn of that year. He succeeded in moving the craft about the lake much faster than by hand, and more to his amusement and satisfaction. This induced him to employ Symington to put an engine into a larger boat, on the Forth and Clyde Canal. This craft was constructed by putting two boats side by side, and having but one wheel placed between them, thus forming a double boat instead of triple.[1] The next year, December 26, 1789 (the year after Read commenced his improvements, it will be noticed), Miller tried his boat upon the canal. They applied their steam force to it, and it is related, succeeded in driving it at the rate of seven miles per hour, a speed not before attained.[2] This, however, must have been the result of a short and violent effort, beyond the capacity of the boat and machinery, for we learn that both kept breaking and coming to pieces, until the boat was in danger of sinking, and they run her ashore. Miller quarreled with his engineer respecting it, took out the machinery, and gave up any further experiments in steam navigation. It does not appear how his engine was constructed; but it is evident, if Symington had invented such new machinery as to adapt the steam-

1 Woodcroft's *History of Early Steam Navigation.* Woolhouse, p. 31.
2 Woodcroft.

engine to boats, he would have made it a prominent point in the account of his experiment. Let his engine be what it may, the very form of his boats, and mode of applying his propelling force, were fatal to a successful navigation. Instead of moving one boat with two wheels, he substantially undertook to move two boats with one wheel; and when we consider the obstruction his double boat would meet with, from the dead water to be dragged along between the hulks, it is evident it could not possess much power or speed; nor did it possess that combination of machinery in any respect necessary to success. To show the correctness of this position, Symington afterwards,[1] with ten or twelve years' experience added to his profession, was employed by Lord Dundas (in 1801) to build a steam towboat on the same Forth and Clyde Canal, which he called the *Charlotte Dundas;* and this boat did not exceed on the average three and a half miles per hour; and the experiment was given up.

Indeed steam navigation was not introduced into Europe for several years after it had been invented and put in successful operation in the United States. The first boat built outside of this country, which can properly claim the name and character of a steamboat, was built in Great Britain by one of Fulton's workmen, Henry Bell, at his own cost and risk, and put in operation on the Clyde at Glasgow, in 1812.[2] This boat called the *Comet,* was only forty feet long, and carried twenty-five tons, with a four-horse engine, and run as a passenger boat between Glasgow and Green-

1 *Life of Watt,* p. 332. Woodcroft *On Steam Navigation,* p. 55. 1848.
2 Woolhouse, vol. i. p. 470.

ock. British writers attempt to lionize Bell, and make him the true inventor of the steamboat. Woolhouse says:[1] —

"Bell sent a description of the method of applying steam in propelling vessels against wind and tide, to all the emperors and crowned heads of Europe, and also to America, which last government put it in practice in the year 1806."

The above paragraph is recorded in an English work designed as a standard authority, and as the author himself styles it, "a splendid national work." But most surely the United States government was never indebted to Bell for its steamboats; it had not then been much of a steamboat-builder; and we must be allowed to question its "practice" of building them after Bell's plans, or the plans of any one else, as early as 1806, before they came into use at all. The learned author, however, has the candor to remark, that—

"British genius and industry have not been extinguished by transplanting to another climate. The projects of the Americans are seldom founded on the sober reasoning of science. Time will, however, check this evil, and he may expect them to hold that rank in the new world, which Britain has held with so much honor for centuries in the older portion."

And he adds, —

"Considering the importance to America of navigating her immense rivers, it is not surprising that the application of the power of steam to propelling vessels, should by persevering efforts have been first carried into successful practice in that continent."

[1] Renwick *On the Steam-engine*, p. 277.

Woolhouse, however, does not proceed to attribute to any special cause our invention of the cotton gin, nail machine, card machine, block machine, and machine for turning irregular forms, and other inventions and discoveries too numerous to mention, — saying nothing of the great discoveries in electricity by Franklin, and of the magnetic telegraph by Morse, inventions that place this above all other countries for its inventive genius and improvement in the mechanic arts.

As we descend from Woolhouse's "National Work," to the current literature of England, we find repeated instances of British writers, in attempting to attach to their countrymen the credit of this invention.

An article in the "London Journal of the Society of Arts" will suffice as a sample. It was published in that leading English journal of art as late as 1853. It says, "The steamboat was Watt's invention, and about a score of years ago (which would be 1833[1]) it was first put in practice in Scotland, whence it spread over the world." Thus, with very little ceremony, the invention of the steamboat, and the vast spread of steam navigation throughout the world, is, by a single paragraph in the "London Journal," added to the laurels of Great Britain. The paragraph lacks nothing but truth to entitle it to credit and make it complete upon the face of it; but the assumption is so notoriously extravagant as to be innocent of harm.

It is also claimed in England, that Robert Fulton, in

1 The writer of the above article was unfortunate in placing his invention and first experiment with a steamboat, twenty-six years after Fulton put his boat upon the Hudson, and long after boats were introduced the world over!

1804, inspected Symington's boat, *Charlotte Dundas*, and got his ideas of river navigation, with plans and drawings, from him.[1] Symington's and Fulton's boats and machinery scarcely resembled each other; and Fulton had ordered his machinery of Boulton & Watt, and gave them draughts, long before he ever saw Symington's boat.[2]

The "London Quarterly Review" (vol. xix. p. 353), to make it appear that Great Britain should have the credit of inventing the steamboat, says, "Miller, of Dalswinton, in 1787, published a book on applying paddle-wheels with cranks to move boats on canals, and suggested using a steam-engine to turn the cranks; and that Miller transmitted a copy of this book to General Washington."

Miller's triple-boat, built of three skiffs placed side by side, with wheels between them, and cranks turned by the hands of his servants, was used to amuse his children in a safe way, on a small lake or pond.[3] It appears that he made a drawing of this boat and published a description of it,[4] with his men tugging away at the cranks. His description of this thing, is the book referred to in the "London Quarterly," as proof that a steamboat had been built at that date in Great Britain. Neither steam nor the steam-engine had anything to do with this craft when Miller published his book or description of it. It does not appear from the "Review" that he published any book after his disastrous experiments with steam. That he sent a copy

[1] Renwick *On the Steam-engine*, p. 285.

[2] On this subject see *post*.

[3] *Ante*. [4] Muirhead's *Life of Watt*, p. 332.

of his book to Washington, might have been true: as the war between the two countries had closed, and the animosity which the British people and government had entertained against us had partially ceased. If Miller ever sent a copy of his book to Washington, containing a scientific description and drawing of his craft! it would seem that the latter would have suggested the subject to Rumsey or Fitch, both of whom at that time were soliciting his aid and advice in their steamboat projects.

It is also said that Bell furnished Fulton with plans and drawings in 1806;[1] this is disproved also by the fact, that Fulton had closed his experiments at Paris in 1803, and ordered his engine in 1804, with drawings and directions as to the manner of constructing it.[2] In fact, Symington's boat differed from Fulton's so essentially as to bear no comparison; while Bell, instead of furnishing a pattern to Fulton, built his own boat in 1812, after Fulton's.

The zeal of English writers to attach the honor of this invention to their own country, is very natural; but they fail to produce any decisive impression on the intelligent public. That many experiments were made in England as well as in France, tending to accomplish that end, is very certain; but that it was finally accomplished by American genius, and in American waters, is allowed by universal consent.

[1] Renwick, p. 288.

[2] Muirhead's *Life of Watt*, p. 334.

CHAPTER V.

We will now change the scene of these experiments from the opposite side of the Atlantic to our own shores, and trace the progress of this invention in the United States.

James Rumsey, a native of Maryland, and John Fitch of Windsor, Connecticut, were the first in America who made the attempt to propel boats by steam. They were sharp competitors in the project of applying steam to river navigation ; and were engaged simultaneously in their experiments. Their machinery, however, with which they proposed to propel their boats, was very different both in plan and construction from each other. The first effort made by Rumsey, he did not apply steam as the motive power. His boat was constructed with two keels, having a wheel between them, which he designed to move by the force of the current alone, and to which he attached setting poles by means of a shaft, and cranks to work them ; hence he calculated his boat would go best against a pretty swift current ; and as may be seen where there was no current it would not move at all.[1] This curious theory, however, was soon abandoned, after his attempt to reduce it to practice ; but in justice to Rumsey it is proper to say that he intended the boat to run against the currents of rapid rivers only.[2] This experiment was in 1784. He afterwards constructed a boat to be

[1] *Documentary History of New York*, vol. ii. p. 1014. [2] *Ibid.*

propelled by steam; and in December 1787, tried it upon the Potomac, at Bath, Berkeley County, Virginia.[1] He had but very indifferent success, moved his boat but a short distance, and the season closing the river, his boat was laid up, and he made no further experiment with it. The next year he went to England to prosecute his steam projects there; and suddenly died with apoplexy, as he was about to address a crowded audience at Liverpool on the subject.[2]

Rumsey's steamboat was constructed essentially after the plan of Bournelli, being a mode of propelling a vessel by forcing water out at the stern by the power of steam, through a trunk which extended aft from near the bow.[3] Rumsey probably obtained the idea from Dr. Franklin, who was his friend and patron. Franklin, during his residence in France, had taken the opportunity to look into scientific matters of this sort as well as others, and became acquainted with Bournelli's plan.[4] He returned from France in August 1785, and in December following laid a plan of a steamboat before the Philosophical Society at Philadelphia, substantially after that plan, and similar to that which Rumsey afterwards constructed. The water was drawn into the forward end of the trunk from under the boat by means of a pump or cylinder, with the piston worked by the engine — the pump containing a valve that opened and closed to draw in the water and force it into the trunk and out at the stern.[5]

John Fitch, as early as 1785, commenced his steam-

[1] *Documentary History of New York*, vol. ii. p. 1020.

[2] Hows' *History of Virginia*. *Life of Fitch*, p. 374.

[3] See Fig. No. 7. [4] Sparks' *Life of Franklin*, vol. vi. p. 479.

[5] *Documentary History of New York*, vol. ii. p. 1018.

No. 7

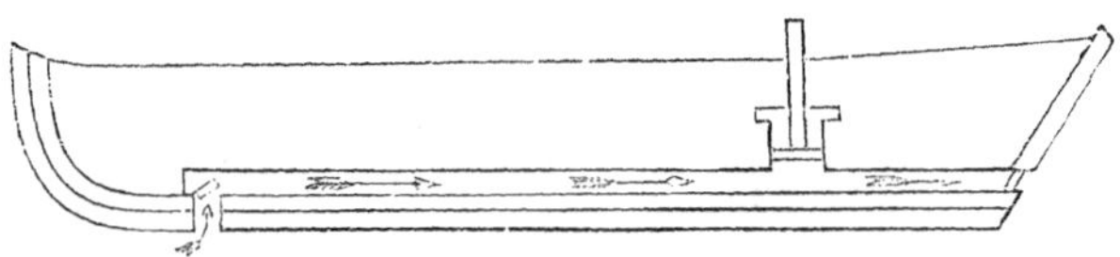

No. 8

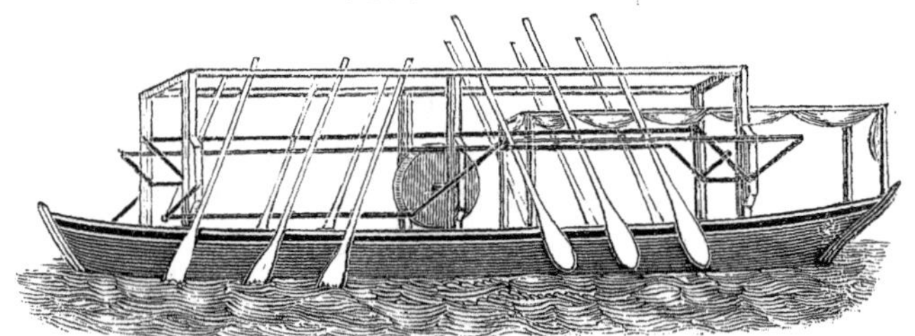

boat projects,[1] being the next year after Rumsey made the attempt to navigate the Potomac against its current, with his water-propelling boat. He thus became a rival of Rumsey in the purpose of river navigation — the object they both then had in view. They entered into a bitter controversy on the question of priority, each claiming to be the first to propose steam power to the propulsion of boats.[2] They not only claimed priority as it respected each other, but as to the whole world. Fitch says "he never heard of such a thing as a steam-engine before he had conceived the idea of one," which was in the spring of that year in which he commenced his steamboat projects, — 1785.[3] And he says moreover, "The propelling of a boat with steam is as new as the rowing of a boat with angels, and I claim the first thought and invention of it." [4]

With these two confessions of Fitch, showing his entire ignorance of the mechanism of the steam-engine, or of any attempt by others to apply it to boats, when he began, it is certainly remarkable that he succeeded as well as he did in his experiments. He says moreover, in a petition to Congress, as late as July, 1790, in referring to his former experiments, — "That his loss of time and money was occasioned by his total ignorance of the improved state of the steam-engine, for not a person could be found who was acquainted with the minutiæ of Boulton & Watt's new engines; and whether your petitioner's engine is similar or not to those in England, he is at this moment totally ignorant." [5]

1 Westcott's *Life of Fitch*, p. 119.
2 *Documentary History of New York*, p. 1012, and *post.*
3 Westcott's *Life of Fitch*, p. 119.
4 *Ibid.* p. 172. 5 *Ibid.* p. 299.

From the above statements of Fitch, it is evident, he knew little or nothing of the great improvements of Watt upon the steam-engine, or of any just method of adapting it to steam navigation.

Fitch first proposed to build his boat after the plan of Bournelli, as presented by Franklin to the Philosophical Society; and ordered the hull to be built on that plan,[1] — of course with a double kelson. But Henry Voight, whom he had employed to assist him in building his engine, persuaded him to give up that plan for some other mode of propulsion; but proposed as the first object to build their engine.

Fitch & Voight accordingly went to work and constructed a small engine for a model, of only one-inch cylinder.[2] But it had not sufficient force to overcome the friction, and give it self motion. They then made one with a three-inch cylinder, and tried a small skiff by hand with paddles, and one or two other modes, none of which gave them satisfaction. This experiment was in July, 1786.[3] Soon after the above trial he applied cranks to his oars or paddles, and found that they worked better. They then put the engine into the skiff, and the experiment was sufficiently satisfactory to induce a part of the company who were aiding Fitch, to believe that a boat of larger size might be safely built.

There is no very definite means of knowing the nature of the engine they used. It however appears that it had a double-acting cylinder and cranks; that "each stroke of the piston turned the axle-tree about two thirds round, and each revolution of the axle-tree moved twelve oars, six on a side, with three up and three

[1] *Life of Fitch*, p. 157. [2] *Ibid.* p. 158. [3] *Ibid.* p. 159.

down, rising and falling about five and a half feet."[1] The oars worked perpendicularly and made a stroke downward into the water like the paddles of a canoe."[2] It does not appear that they used the fly-wheel to carry the motion beyond the dead points of the crank, or that the several parts of the engine were properly proportioned to each other — which, as they worked without any formula, could not by anything other than accident, have been the case. The caps of the cylinders were made of wood, and neither these nor the piston could be made air-tight. They used a condenser invented by Voight, which he called the "pipe condenser." Several other forms of condensers were tried and flung aside; the steam valves worked badly;[3] the boiler was of very large size compared with the rest of the engine; said to hold five hundred gallons of water, while the engine and boiler occupied about two thirds the length and size of the boat. It was calculated the boiler and other machinery would weigh from five to seven tons, beside fuel; while the boat was but forty-five feet long and twelve feet beam.[4] Yet they succeeded in moving this craft when under full way, from three to four miles per hour, but frequent stoppages were made to accumulate fresh supplies of steam and repair the engine: "for as one defect was remedied another became apparent."[5] All this makes it quite evident that they had not hit very near Watt, in the construction of their

1 See Fig. No. 8. 2 *Life of Fitch*, p. 177.

3 Westcott's *Life of Fitch*, p. 185, and *post.*

4 See affidavits of William Askew and Henry Bedinger, *Documentary History of New York*, vol. ii. pp. 1024, 1025. 5 *Life of Fitch*, p. 186.

engine or made any improvement in the massive boiler, to fit it for steam navigation. This experiment was in July and August 1787.

No further experiments were made with the above described boat, but it was abandoned and a new boat built sixty feet long and eight feet beam, in 1788; and the machinery of the old boat taken out and put into this; at the same time the oars of the old boat were dispensed with and substituted by three or four paddles, much broader than the oars, and used at the stern, instead of the sides of the boat.[1] They went from Philadelphia to Burlington, twenty miles, and the boiler sprung a leak just as they arrived at the latter place. This was the first trip of that distance ever made by a steamboat known in history, which was the last of July or 1st of August 1788.[2] They repaired up the boat and made three or four trips that fall to Burlington, on an average speed of about four miles per hour. This speed did not meet the expectations of the company, and most of them, with Voight, gave up the project.[3]

Fitch however got up another company in the spring of 1789, and began another boat with an eighteen-inch cylinder. A condenser invented by Dr. Thornton was put into it; they then tried Voight's pipe condenser with no better success. These changes occupied the summer, but in December they tried the new boat, after enlarging the air-pump. Yet this boat succeeded no better than the old one, and it was laid up for the winter.[4] In the spring following, 1790, they tried

[1] *Life of Fitch*, p. 248, and *post*.
[2] *Ibid.* p. 250.
[3] *Ibid.* p. 252.
[4] *Ibid*, p. 270, and *post*.

another sort of condenser, and wholly failed to work the boat. This was the seventh condenser they had experimented with, all of different construction and of their own getting up — clearly showing how they worked in the dark, without any specific knowledge of the steam-engine as improved by Watt. Another condenser of Fitch's contrivance, however, was tried; and on the 16th of April, as Fitch expressed himself, "They reigned Lord High Admirals of the Delaware."[1] The boat run on the average about six miles per hour; and now and then was brought up to the speed of seven or eight miles. It was run as a passenger boat between Philadelphia and Trenton three months or so;[2] but from the crude and imperfect character of the machinery, the ill adaptation of one part to the other, the clumsy working of the paddles behind, the great expense of fuel, and the little space on the boat except what the engine, boiler, and fuel occupied, the attention required to keep it in repair, as the machinery kept continually getting out of order, and the expenses of running the boat constantly accumulating beyond its earnings, all together, made it a losing business, and it was abandoned.[3]

The difficulties Fitch labored under, not only from his own lack of information, as to the true philosophical data and structure of the steam-engine, and the perplexities he constantly met, while groping in the dark to construct his machinery, were made apparent in this experiment. Nevertheless, it is a fact that Fitch, with machinery that never could be profitably or successfully applied to navigation, even upon the rivers, fored

1 *Life of Fitch*, p. 281. 2 *Ibid.* 284, and *post.* 3 *Ibid.* p. 285.

his boat at a greater speed than did Fulton in his first experiment upon the Hudson; but Fulton had got upon the right track, where his path was felicitous and smooth; while Fitch rushed headlong against fatal and unforeseen obstacles.

Fitch made some feeble attempts to renew his experiments, but without success. He quarreled with Voight and his friends, who had now lost their confidence in him, and he could raise no funds but now and then a few dollars out of pity to relieve him of his extreme necessities. Thus far his career had been of a remarkable character, just such as would be likely to follow the efforts of such a man. He combined with a rare and remarkable genius, qualities that were fatal to his success. His genius had to contend with his ignorance, excitable temper, and intemperate habits, — an array of difficulties that it could not overcome. He was ever groping in the dark, urged on by his impulses, and thus subjected himself to a life of successive calamities. He had conceived the idea of a steam-engine, and of its results when applied to boats, as he says; and set himself to work to build one and make the application. His plans and drawings, taken from his own crude mind for the most part, were necessarily vague and imperfect; and the machinery forged from them would work badly or not at all, perplex him, and discourage his employers.

Had Fitch taken the same pains that George Stephenson did — who at the age of eighteen could neither read nor write — to acquire an intimate knowledge of his profession, and direct his genius by scientific principles, his career no doubt would have been equally successful and glorious. Success would have raised him above himself, kept down his petulance and ill-temper, and overcome the evils of dissipation; it would have made a man of him, as he felt himself to be, when he "reigned Lord High Admiral of the Delaware." He had in the very character of the men who gave him their patronage, a basis for all the material aid he required: they were anxious to furnish the means, but they wanted the assurance that they would not be spent in vain. Fitch was not the man to give them this assurance. As it was, however, the honest-hearted fellow labored not in vain; he accomplished more in driving his boat, crude as it was, than had ever been done before; but he fell far short of introducing to the world a practicable mode of navigation by steam.

This man of genius and misfortune, after spending some years in poverty and distress, took up his residence at Bardstown, Kentucky, where by his own hand he flung off this mortal coil, — closing a life of perseverance, intermixed with bitter disappointment and trouble. Before his death he made the request, "that he should be buried on the banks of the Ohio, that he might repose where the song of the boatman would enliven the stillness of his resting-place, and the music of the steam-engine soothe his spirit." [1] Truly prophetic words!

[1] Hows' *History of Virginia.*

CHAPTER VI.

It has been noticed that Read as early as 1788, while a resident of Salem, devoted himself to the purpose of applying steam-power to navigation and land transport. Having learned the unsuccessful attempts made by Rumsey upon the Potomac, and Fitch upon the Delaware in 1787, and believing that their failure was owing to their ill-constructed machinery, and modes of propulsion, he sought to overcome the difficulty, by the invention and combination of machinery of a different and more perfect kind. He believed this could be done by so modifying Watt's improved engine as to fit it for a *portable* as well as *stationary* power. It had thus far been used in mills or fixed localities, where it was expected to remain, and it had been invented for no other purpose. Thus its heft and bulk hardly came into account in its construction. Indeed, power and durability were the great objects, without regard to size or weight in the stationary engines; but not so in an engine to be used in a boat or land carriage. In both of these cases they must not only be of small size, but light, and so light as to be carried in the craft or carriage they propel, not only with convenience and ease, but with economy and profit. In short, the engine must be of small size, comparatively light, without any loss of power, and work with freedom and safety. He believed, moreover, that the modes of propulsion used by Rumsey and Fitch — setting-poles, oars, paddles, or the ejection of water from the stern of the boat — were not only awkward in their operation but unreliable.

His first and great purpose was to invent a new boiler, of such a character as to dispense with the massive, old-fashioned boilers, and thus reduce the engine several tons' weight. He succeeded in the invention of a boiler, of which he made draughts and constructed a model, differing entirely from any before known or in use, which, from its characteristic principles, he denominated the "Portable Furnace Boiler." To use his own words, "it occupied but little space, was light and strong, and so constructed as to require no other furnace than what itself constituted, and was designed both for boats and land carriages." This boiler was constructed of seventy-eight tubes, placed within it, and hence has been generally denominated the tubular, or more properly, the *multi-tubular, boiler*.[1] The model of this boiler is not to be found, and is supposed to have been consumed in 1836, when

[1] The tubes were placed in a vertical position, as will be seen from the following plan and specification of it. In the use of the multi-tubular boiler placed in this position, the *Encyclopædia Britannica* (vol. xx. p. 651), revised and republished the present year, 1860, speaks as follows: —

"The Americans have adopted a form of tubular boiler, in which the tubes are disposed vertically, the smoke and flame passing round the outside of the tubes, and the water being contained in the inside. These vertical-tube boilers are very effective in generating steam, and partly for this reason, that the flame reaches further amongst their tubes than in the case of a horizontal boiler, in consequence of the greater space outside the tubes in which the flame may develop itself. The importance of this, especially while using the flaming bituminous coal, is very great. The absorbent surface is greater, and the weight of water it is necessary to carry is much less."

the Patent Office was destroyed by fire. The following copies of the patent, specification, and drawings of the boiler will sufficiently describe its form and nature. The patent also includes an improvement of the steam cylinder and method of propelling boats by means of the chain-wheel, which I shall notice hereafter.[1]

"THE UNITED STATES

"*To all to whom these presents shall come*

"GREETING:

"Whereas, Nathan Read, of Salem, in the State of Massachusetts, hath presented a petition to the Secretary of State, the Secretary of the Department of War, and the Attorney-General of the United States, alleging and suggesting that he hath discovered the following useful devices, not before known neither used; that is to say, an improvement of the boiler of the steam-engine, by constructing it in such a manner as to constitute of itself a complete furnace that more effectually prevents the loss of heat than any other furnace that is wholly or in part foreign to the boiler itself, — by reducing its size, and rendering it very portable, and at the same time increasing its force, by exposing within a small space a very large surface directly to the fire, and by connecting it with a reservoir in such a way as to be replenished with water with as much safety and convenience when on board a vessel in motion as at rest. Also an improvement of the steam cylinder, by which it is rendered more portable and convenient for working in an inclined or horizontal position, and which is in the piston, which has two stems, or rods, one coming out at each end of the cylinder, and alternately acting with equal force and in contrary directions. And also a practical mode of driving or impelling

[1] The original papers in the family of Judge Read.

boats or vessels of any kind in the water or against the current, by means of the chain-wheel, or rowing machine, constructed and operating upon the general principles of the chain-pump, and moved by the force of steam or any other power, in the same manner the chain-pump is moved; and praying that a patent may be granted therefor. And whereas, the said discovery hath been deemed sufficiently useful and important: These are, therefore, in pursuance of the Act entitled 'An Act to promote the Progress of the Useful Arts,' to grant to the said Nathan Read, his heirs, administrators, or assigns, for the term of fourteen years, the sole and exclusive right of making, using, and vending to others to be used, the said discovery, so far as he, the said Nathan Read was the discoverer, according to the allegations and suggestions of the said petition.

"In testimony whereof I have caused these Letters to be made Patent, and the Seal of the United States to be hereunto affixed.

"Given under my hand, at the City of Philadelphia, this twenty-sixth day of August, in the year of our Lord one thousand seven hundred and ninety-one, and of the Independence of the United States of America the sixteenth.

"GEORGE WASHINGTON.

[L. S.] "By the President,

"THOS. JEFFERSON.

"CITY OF PHILADELPHIA, *Aug.* 26, 1791.

"I do hereby certify that the foregoing Letters-patent were delivered to me in pursuance of an Act entitled 'An Act to promote the Progress of the Useful Arts;' that I have examined the same, and find them conformable to said Act. "EDM. RANDOLPH, *Attorney-General.*"

"SPECIFICATION OF AN IMPROVED STEAM-BOILER.

"PLATE I.

"Fig. 1 shows a perspective view of the boiler.

"Fig. 2 a vertical section of its parts.

"Fig. 3 a horizontal section through the mouth of the furnace.

"Fig. 4 a horizontal section of the upper part of the furnace.

"The letters of reference are made to answer to the same parts in all the figures in this plate. *A*, the fuel door, covering the mouth of the furnace, which is represented by a dotted circle. *B B*, the reservoir from which the boiler is replenished with water through the pipe *D*, which has a stop-cock to close it after the boiler is replenished. *C*, a tube, with a stop-cock, through which the reservoir is filled. This tube should be shut while the tubes *D* and *N* are open. To replenish the boiler, shut the tube *C* and open *D* and *N*. *E*, the funnel which conveys the smoke from the furnace. The funnel is conveyed through the reservoir, that the water may be hot before it enters the boiler. *F*, the steam-pipe that conveys off the steam from the boiler as fast as it is generated. *G G*, Fig. 2, a cylindrical vessel forming the external part of the boiler. *H H*, a smaller cylindrical vessel forming the inner part of the boiler and external part of the furnace. The cylindrical vessels are united at bottom, as represented in Fig. 2 and in the model. *I I*, the top of the furnace, perforated to receive the long tubes *a a a*, etc., which are open at both ends, and also to receive the short tubes *b b b*, etc., which are open at top and closed at bottom. *K K*, the bottom of the furnace, perforated to receive the long tubes *a a a*, etc., represented by the dotted circles in Fig. 3. *L*, that part of the furnace that contains the fuel.

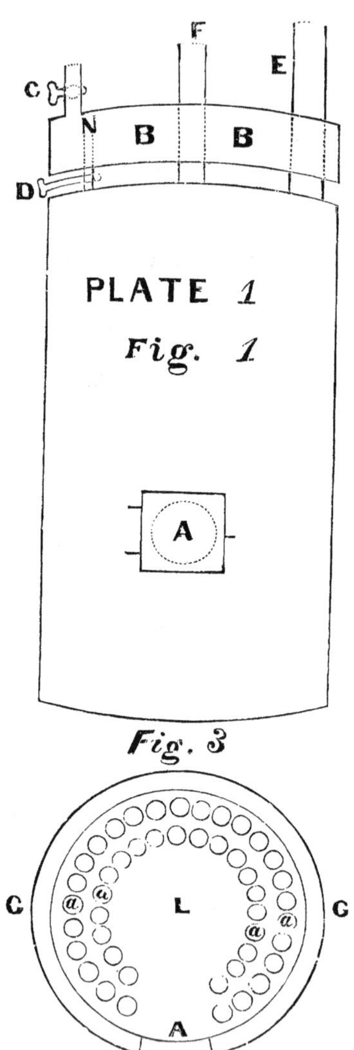

C
N
B
B
F
E
D
PLATE 1
Fig. 1
A
Fig. 3
C
a
a
L
a
a
C
A

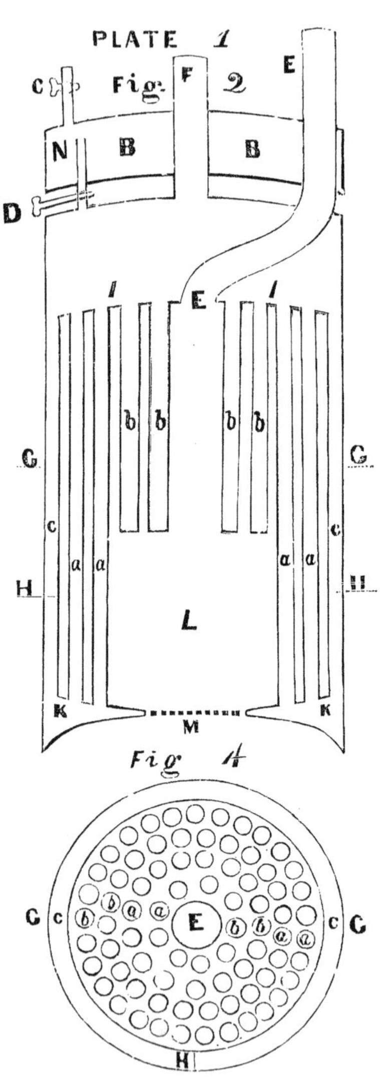

PLATE 1
Fig 2
C
F
E
N
B
B
D
E
b b b b
G
G
c
c
a a a a
H
H
L
K
K
M
Fig 4
E
b a a
b
b b a a
C c
c C
H

M, an opening on the bottom of the boiler, through which the air passes up into the furnace and feeds the flame. The grate is placed in this opening, as represented in Fig. 2. The number of tubes and size of the boiler may be increased or diminished at pleasure. The boiler should be made of copper or iron, and all its parts well brazed or riveted together, in the same manner in which work of this kind is commonly done. The boiler, like all others, should have a valve to give the steam vent should it be in danger of bursting.

" *To all to whom these presents shall come:*

" I, NATHAN READ of Salem, in the State of Massachusetts, being the grantee of a Patent from the United States, for several improvements by me discovered, not known or used before such discovery, in applications of steam to useful purposes; do by these presents deliver to the Secretary of State the specifications hereto annexed, of the discovery aforesaid, in pursuance of the Act entitled 'An Act to promote the progress of the Useful Arts.' Given under my hand and seal in the office of the Secretary of State this twenty-third day of April, in the year of our Lord one thousand seven hundred and ninety-one.

"NATHAN READ." [L. S.]

The above specification with corresponding drawings present a lucid and intelligent description of this remarkable invention; but no less remarkable in its conception than important in its results. The boiler alone actually prepared the steam-engine for a utility that it never before possessed. It rendered it portable, and made it a practical agent for moving boats and land carriages. It is claimed by the friends of Judge Read, that this was the first multi-tubular boiler invented; and this was what the inventor himself claimed, as will hereafter appear, and as shown not only by the foregoing patent which he received as the original inventor, but by the following extract of a letter by him to Mr. Jefferson, then Secretary of State, and by virtue of his office one of the Commissioners of Patents: —

"SALEM, *January 8th*, 1791.

"SIR: — I forwarded last week to Mr. Remsen[1] models of several machines, drafts and descriptions of which are inclosed. The model of the boiler which I have forwarded, is an improvement upon one of those I exhibited last winter. The model I refer to consists of several annular vessels placed one above another within the furnace, in such a manner as to expose a very large surface directly to the fire. For annular vessels, placed in a horizontal position, I have substituted circular tubes, placed in a vertical position[2] within the furnace, which is formed by the boiler itself in the same manner as the other was. In the last boiler, which is stronger, more simple and elegant in its construction, I have paid less regard to the evaporating surface than in either of the others — finding by experiment that the principle of evaporation suggested by your Excellency is perfectly just, when applied to close vessels. I am sensible that a pipe was several years since made use of by Mr. Rumsey for generating steam, and also perceive from the 'Philosophical Transactions,' that a tube in the form of the worm of a still was used upwards of twenty years ago for the same purpose; *but do not know that any other person but myself hath ever*

1 Mr. Remsen was the Secretary of the Board of Commissioners.

2 In the *Scientific American*, vol. iii. No. 11, new series, p. 174, September 8, 1860, the editors say, "The reason why we prefer a boiler with vertical tubes, is owing to the favorable results which have been obtained with such a boiler on board the United States frigate *San Jacinto* in comparison with one having the old-fashioned tubes. We do not mean one that has the fire returned through the tubes; but water tubes, as explained in Isherwood's *Engineering Precedents*."

constructed a tubular boiler, formed in such a manner as to constitute of itself a complete furnace. It is about three years since I first projected a boiler upon this plan. How far my improvements merit an exclusive privilege, the Honorable Board will judge. Should a Patent be granted, I suggest it may be delivered to Benjamin Goodhue, Esq., who will pay Mr. Remsen all charges that have arisen in consequence of my application.

"I am, with the sincerest respect,

"Your Excellency's most obedient servant,

"NATHAN READ."

In Woolhouse's edition of "Tredgold," vol. i. p. 413, he says: —

"The introduction of tubes into the boiler, is one of the greatest improvements that has been made in the construction of locomotives, and was the cause of the superiority of the Rocket engine to those that competed with it, and to all the former engines. The Rocket engine made by Mr. R. Stephenson, which was the engine that gained the prize for the best locomotive, at the opening of the Liverpool and Manchester Railway, in 1829, was the first engine made with tubes in this country."

And in a note on the same page he adds:[1] —

"It appears that the merit of the first invention of a boiler with tubes is due to a French engineer, M. Seguin, who had a patent for it in 1828; although the application of the principle in the Rocket engine was undoubtedly an independent invention."

The above allusions to the invention of the "multi-tubular boiler"[2] were undoubtedly made without a knowledge of Read's invention and patent of it.

[1] Woolhouse, vol. i. p. 413.

[2] This is the proper name of the boiler.

But by comparison the general principles of this and the boiler of the "Rocket" will be found to resemble each other sufficiently to be the result of one and the same invention; and Read's invention was more than forty years anterior to either Seguin's or Stephenson's experiments. The only perceptible difference lay in the fact, that this boiler of Read was intended to carry the water through the tubes and the fire through the cavities between them; while Stephenson's boiler carried the fire through the tubes and the water through the cavities — a change very simple and easily made, and no doubt an improvement for locomotive engines; and it will hereafter appear that Read proposed the same thing — in short that he invented the multi-tubular boiler, to be used in either form, *i. e.*, one with the flame passing through the tubes, and the other with the water.

To show the analogy between the boiler invented by Read and that used upon the "Rocket" at the celebrated trial at Rainhill, the following description of the boiler of the "Rocket" used on that occasion, prepared by that eminent engineer, Robert Stephenson (son of George Stephenson), who under the direction of his father built the "Rocket" and obtained the prize, may be regarded as the best evidence that can be obtained on the subject. He says:—

"At this stage of the locomotive engine, we have in the multi-tubular boiler the only important principle of construction introduced, in addition to those which my father had brought to bear at a very early age (between the years 1814 and 1821), on the Killingworth Colliery Railway.[1] In the

[1] Stephenson built his first locomotive at Killingworth in 1814. "The

'Rocket' engine the power of generating steam was prodigiously increased by the adoption of the multi-tubular boiler. Its efficiency was further augmented by narrowing the orifice by which the waste steam escaped into the chimney; for by this means the velocity of the air in the chimney, or in other words the draught of the fire, was increased to an extent that far surpassed the expectations even of those who had been the authors of the combination. From the date of running the 'Rocket' on the Liverpool and Manchester Railway, the locomotive engine has received many improvements in detail, and especially in accuracy of workmanship; but in no essential particular does the existing locomotive differ from that (the 'Rocket') which obtained the prize in the celebrated competition at Rainhill.

"In this instance, as in every other important step in science and art, various claimants have arisen for the merit of having suggested the multi-tubular boiler as a means of obtaining the necessary heating surface. Whatever may be the value of their respective claims, the public, useful, and extensive application of the invention must certainly date from the experiments made at Rainhill. M. Seguin, for whom engines had been made by my father some years previously, states that he patented a similar multi-tubular boiler in France, several years before.[1]

boiler was cylindrical, eight feet in length and thirty-four inches in diameter, with an internal flue-tube twenty inches wide passing through it. The engine had two vertical cylinders of eight inches and two feet stroke let into the boiler, working the propelling gear with cross-heads and connecting rods." He used spur-wheels and had a chamber around the chimney to heat the water before it entered the boiler. His car-wheels were all of a smooth surface, which he found by experiment were sufficient for traction. *Life of Stephenson*, p. 90, *post.*

[1] George Stephenson sent two engines to France in 1828 for the St. Etienne Railway constructed in his usual form. Seguin took out Stephenson's boilers, and applied others with the flame passing through the tubes, which greatly increased the power of the engines. This gave Stephenson the idea of that form of boiler, which he afterwards applied to the "Rocket."

"A still prior claim is made by Mr. Stevens of New York, who was all but the rival of Mr. Fulton in the introduction of steamboats on the American rivers. It is stated as early as 1807 he used the multi-tubular boiler. These claimants may all be entitled to great and independent merit; but certain it is that the perfect establishment of the success of the multi-tubular boiler is more immediately due to the suggestion of Mr. Henry Booth, and to my father's practical knowledge in carrying it out.[1]

"The boiler of the 'Rocket' was cylindrical with flat ends, six feet in length and three feet four inches in diameter. The upper half of the boiler was used as a reservoir for the steam, the lower half being filled with water. Through the lower part, twenty-five copper tubes of three inches diameter extended, which were opened to the fire-box at one end, and to the chimney at the other. The fire-box or furnace, two feet wide and three feet high, was attached immediately behind the boiler, and was also surrounded with water. The cylinders were placed on each side of the boiler, in an oblique position, one end being nearly level with the top of the boiler at its after end, and the other pointing towards the centre of the foremost or driving pair of wheels; with which the connection was directly made from the piston-rod to a pin on the outside of the wheel. The engine and water weighed four and a quarter tons, and was supported on four wheels not coupled. The tender was four wheeled,

And from this circumstance its invention was imputed to Seguin. *Life of Stephenson*, p. 262.

[1] *Life of George Stephenson*, by Smiles, p 263.

Henry Booth, secretary of the Liverpool and Manchester Railway, proposed to Stephenson to apply the boiler of Seguin to the "Rocket" engine, and the multi-tubular boiler, as they called it, was thereupon adopted. Booth was interested with Stephenson in the construction of the "Rocket." *Ibid.*

and similar in shape to a wagon; the foremost part holding the fuel and the hind part a water cask."[1]

The priority and rights of the respective claimants to the invention of the multi-tubular boiler, will be more particularly noticed hereafter; for the present the reader is invited to compare the above description of the boiler of the "Rocket" with the specification and drawings of Read of his boiler, which he patented in 1791 (*ante*, p. 48); from which it will appear that the principles of their construction were essentially the same. In the mean time, to show the advantage of the multi-tubular boiler over every other mode proposed, we will here give a brief account of the trial at Rainhill of the several engines entered for the prize.

The prize offered by the Liverpool and Manchester Railway Company was £500 to the most successful locomotive, the speed not to average less than ten miles an hour, the engine to consume its own smoke, not to be of more than six tons weight, and be able to draw twenty tons day by day; the boiler to have two safety-valves, one out of the control of the engineer; the engine and boiler to be supported on springs, the engines to be at the Liverpool end of the line ready for trial on the 1st of October, 1829. Each engine was to run two miles (the track being level), and make twenty trips in a day, and each to run on different days. The engines entered were as follows: the "Novelty," constructed by Messrs. Braithwaite & Ericsson; the "Sans-pariel," by Timothy Harkworths; the "Rocket," by Messrs. Stephenson & Booth; the "Perseverance," by Mr. Burstalls.[2]

[1] *Life of Stephenson*, p. 265. [2] *Ibid.* pp. 266, 267.

Stephenson was the first ready and the first to open the course; which, however, was not until the 6th of October. On that day the multitude assembled to witness the strength and speed of the young giants; a scene of intense curiosity, and of far greater interest in the view of all intelligent people, than any exhibition of the mechanic arts which had appeared before the world since the successful opening of steam navigation upon the Hudson. It was not a test of speed resulting from the mechanism of nature, like the tension and force of the muscle and bone and sinew of the horse, but from a force the work of human hands, and owing its creation and existence to human contrivance. A stud of animals about to exhibit their speed upon the race-course would excite but little interest, but for machines constructed by mortal artisans, self-moving and put in motion by fire and water, to enter the race, to speed their way through smoke and flame, upon limbs and joints of steel, was a novel affair. The interest produced by the occasion, most surely, was not greater than the result of the experiment foreboded; a decision was to be made whether the anticipations in this behalf, of men of science and genius, were to triumph, or whether all their deductions and labors were to end in a capital failure, and the actors irretrievably set down as a knot of visionary, delusive men. Moreover, whether the vast ends of trade and commerce and public travel, of the speedy centralization of distant lands and communities into one people and one social position, one neighborhood, one knowledge, one faith, who before knew not each other, were to be realized, or, on the other hand, whether all these high hopes were to be given up as impossible, and lost forever ?

It is hardly necessary to add that all the country around, its commonalty, beauty, and fashion, men of learning, nobility, and most eminent engineers and inventors, one and all, with their hopes and fears, stood by to witness the novel exhibition. What had been practically accomplished by Stephenson in the collieries at Killingworth, and upon the Stockton and Darlington Railway, which he had previously constructed with a degree of success far beyond the expectations of his employers, had partially opened the eyes of the public, and the world of gazers now looked upon the subject, not as a positive delusion of some cracked brain, but with a timid yet wavering sort of faith that seemed hardly to know what it was about, or how to believe its own eyes.

The "Rocket" made its first trial by running six times back and forth over the two-mile track; and it performed this run, being twelve miles, in fifty-three minutes. It then gave the track to the "Novelty," which was next called out; and on this first day it ran at the rate of twenty-four miles per hour, nearly doubling the speed of the "Rocket." The "Novelty" had a bellows attached to its engine to produce combustion, and used an engine and boiler of the ordinary form as constructed by Boulton & Watt. The "Sans-pariel" was next called out, but the day was so far spent that it did not enter upon the track until the next day, when its boiler became defective, and it withdrew from the contest to make amends. On the second day, the bellows of the "Novelty" also gave out, and it hauled off for repairs. The boiler of the "Sans-pariel" was like that of the "Novelty," but it used the steam-blast instead of a bellows to produce combustion. The "Perseverance" came upon the track, but was not able to go beyond six miles per hour, and was withdrawn from the contest. On this day, the "Rocket" was again put to the test. Stephenson hitched an omnibus to it containing thirty persons, and ran with his car-load of passengers at the rate of twenty-four to thirty miles per hour.[1]

The third day, the "Rocket" ran, as its maximum speed, twenty-nine miles per hour, with about thirteen tons' weight attached to the engine, — its speed exceeding so far any previous calculation on the subject, and being so far beyond anything the eyes of the world had ever before seen passing in tractile force before them, that it made the exhibition a matter of wonder and astonishment, as well as enthusiastic admiration. The fourth day, the "Novelty" again appeared upon the track. It passed down well, and indicated a close run with the "Rocket"; but on its return the pipe of its forcing-pump burst, and it was again withdrawn for repairs. It was afterwards placed upon the track, and pressed to its maximum speed; but did not exceed from twenty-four to twenty-eight miles per hour.[2]

On the 13th, the "Sans-pariel," having been placed in repair, once more took the course, oiled up its joints, and fed its fires for a more hopeful showing. It passed up and down the track, but was not able to exceed fourteen miles per hour on the average. At length its pump got out of order, and it was obliged to stop

[1] *Life of Stephenson*, p. 268. [2] *Ibid*, p. 269.

and give up the controversy. The next day, the "Novelty" made another attempt to run; but it broke down, and gave up any further trial. The "Rocket," having in all respects fulfilled, and, indeed, far surpassed the conditions stipulated in the promised reward, received the prize; and after the award Stephenson, with a view to test the actual speed of the "Rocket," and show that he had not yet done what he might do, again put it on the course, disencumbered of any load. To the astonishment of all beholders, he now ran, without accident or delay, at the rate of thirty-five miles per hour; and he publicly declared that a mile a minute, with proper improvements upon the engine, was attainable. It was now, to use the words of Mr. Smiles, that both "foul weather and fair weather friends" joined in eulogizing Stephenson for his success — a success attained by the adoption of the multi-tubular boiler.[1]

It is proper here to notice, that the "Rocket" alone on this occasion, used the multi-tubular boiler. The boilers of the "Novelty" and "Sans-pariel" were both of the same construction, and were of two tubes, or flues, in the form of the letter U, and presented a far less amount of heating surface than that of the "Rocket," which, with the steam-blast, gave to the "Rocket" its superior capacity and advantage, and secured to it the prize.[2] Mr. Smiles, in his "Life of George Stephenson," remarks on this subject: —

[1] *Life of Stephenson*, p. 271.

[2] The steam-blast was produced by conducting the waste steam by a pipe into the chimney, thus increasing the draught and effecting a more intense combustion in the furnace. It was supposed that the power of the engine would diminish as the velocity increased; but Stephenson maintained and

"It was the simple but admirable contrivance of the steam, blast, and its combination with the multi-tubular boiler, with its large heating surface, that at once gave the high-pressure locomotive its vigorous life, and secured the triumph of the railway system. As has been well observed, this wonderful ability to increase and multiply its powers of performance with the emergency that demands them, has made this giant engine the noblest creation of human wit — the very lion among machines." [1]

Smiles does not attribute the invention of the multi-tubular boiler to Stephenson, but concedes that it was invented by some one else.[2] He seems to have had no other information respecting it than the account of Seguin's experiment, to whom, from the simple fact that he was known to use it, he would accede the invention, but without any definite knowledge that he (Seguin) was in truth the actual inventor. It does not appear that Seguin claimed the invention, — he gave Stephenson no such information, — although he took out a patent for it in France, which he had the right to do, and applied it to Stephenson's engines, on the St. Etienne Railway. It is certainly a most remarkable fact, in its relations to the history of that invention, that none of our writers have hitherto been able to put their finger upon the man whom they presumed to say was the actual inventor. It is barely mentioned by some American authors, and referred

proved by experiment that the reverse was the fact — that the more rapid the motion of the engine, the more intense was the combustion. The current of air produced and drawn through the tubes by the current of steam through the chimney (the steam-blast) more than doubled the power of the engine.

[1] *Life of Stephenson*, p. 288.

[2] *Ibid.* p. 261.

to by writers abroad, that Stevens of New York was supposed to be the inventor; but no writer has ever given any facts to support such an assumption. And as the matter now stands before the world, the invention, from the above mere assumptions, without any evidence of that positive kind which the case demands, and which from its very nature it is susceptible of furnishing, is carelessly attributed to Stevens or Seguin — to the former because some one said he claimed it, and to the latter because he used it. By a reference to Read's patent, specification, and drawings, the evidence becomes written and positive, instead of circumstantial and presumptive. The absurdity of Stevens's claims to this invention will more particularly appear when we come to consider the nature of his application to the New York Legislature and the Commissioners of Patents, in his controversy with Rumsey & Fitch. And how it probably came to Seguin's knowledge, will also appear hereafter.

CHAPTER VII.

THE boiler of Read was constructed with special reference to boats and land carriages, and was placed in a vertical position for both; and, as appears from the foregoing note[1] from the "Encyclopædia Britannica," it is a mode very effective, and coming more into use, and may be applied to locomotives as well as boats. The boiler of the locomotive engine, however, has for the most part been used in a horizontal position, with the flame instead of the water passing through the tubes. But the mode of using these boilers, whether vertical or horizontal, is regulated by utility or convenience, as the builder may decide for himself, and is not regarded as any part of the invention. Indeed they may be used in any position, and with the water or flame passing through the tubes at pleasure.

The length and size of the boiler, moreover, is no part of the invention, as it is designed to be longer or shorter, and of greater or less diameter, according to the position in which you intend to place it, and the amount of work you aim to have it perform. So, too, the number of tubes that pass through the boiler is not specifically fixed, but may be more or less as desired. Read's boiler, as appears from the plan (see Plate I., Fig. 4), had seventy-eight. The "Rocket" had but twenty-four, and Stephenson's first locomotive on the

[1] See p. 47.

London and Birmingham Railway, a hundred and twenty-four;[1] and at this day, usually, many more than that are used.[2] The size of the tubes was smaller than those in the "Rocket" (these last being three inches), and larger than those generally used at this day, the inner diameter being, ordinarily, about one and seven-eighths inches, the diameter of the tubes depending, in a great measure, upon the number used and the size of the boiler. It will be seen by the plate (Fig. 2) that the tubes were straight, and fitted into the tube-plates in the same manner as in the "Rocket,"[3] and open at each end, except the short ones over the fire-grate, which were closed at the lower end. That there was also a method of heating the water before it passed into the boiler, — an idea carried out in the boiler of the "Rocket," but in a somewhat different form; the one by conducting the steam-pipe and funnel through the reservoir, and the other by conducting the water along the side of the fire chamber, or box. The boiler was cylindrical in its form, as now used, being the best form for strength;[4] and it had an external and internal cylinder, the latter forming the external part of the furnace, heating, in addition to the tubes, a large surface of water contained between the two cylinders. It was also furnished with pipes to replenish the boiler, and conduct the steam to the cylinder, with suitable cocks and valves to regulate them, and a safety-valve; and the boiler to be made

[1] Woolhouse, vol. i. pp. 412, 413.

[2] Of the main boilers of the *Great Eastern* Steamship, ten in all, four have four hundred tubes, and six have four hundred and twenty each, three inches in diameter.

[3] Woolhouse, vol. i. p. 412, plate xc. [4] *Ibid*, p. 126.

of copper or iron, and all its parts properly brazed or riveted together.

Indeed, it will readily be seen, that by placing Read's boiler in a horizontal position, and conducting the fire through the tubes instead of the small apartments between them, with suitable arrangements to conform to this change, it will in every aspect of it be the same thing as that used in the "Rocket." George Stephenson, the father of Robert, commenced his railroad experiments as early as 1814, and from that time up to 1829, fifteen years, he was unable to run his locomotive beyond seven or eight miles an hour. But in 1829, after introducing the multi-tubular boiler, and the steam-blast, as before noted, he at once increased its speed to thirty-five miles per hour;[1] and by one slight improvement after another, mostly in the workmanship of the machinery, he afterwards brought it up to a maximum speed of sixty miles per hour.[2] The steam-blast, and application of the multi-tubular boiler, are also spoken of "as the two grand inventions of Stephenson's life; and as forming the very soul of the locomotive."[3]

In Smiles's "Life of Stephenson,"— page five of the preface, — he remarks, "The invention of the locomotive engine and its application to the working of railways, is one of the most remarkable events of the present century." And he proceeds to consider, "What manner of men were they by whom this great work was accomplished? How did the conception first

1 Smiles's *Life of George Stephenson*, p. 285.
2 *Westminster Review*, July, 1857, p. 128.
3 *Ibid.*

dawn upon their minds? By what means did railways grow and quicken into such vigorous life? By what moral and material agencies did the inventors and founders of the system work out the ideas whose results have been so prodigious?"

In this excellent work, however, the subject of this memoir finds no place. His great labors upon the steam-engine to prepare it for locomotion, which in point of fact opened the way for Stephenson's subsequent success and triumph, were not known to this apparently impartial author. Had he before him the evidences of Read's inventions and improvements, no doubt he would have given him his proper place in his history of railroad invention; and awarded to him his just claims for the early part he took in working out "the ideas whose results have been so prodigious." And although the distinguished author wrote as a true and loyal subject of a foreign country, there is no reason for imputing to him any wish or desire to conceal the labors or genius of American inventors, — in this respect he seems to take a position far above the fretful prejudice of other English writers on the subject. He does not claim for Stephenson that he was the inventor of the multi-tubular boiler; but on the other hand, frankly admits that he was not; and speaks of Seguin's experiments with it as the first within his knowledge, yet does not claim to assert that Seguin was the inventor of it.

CHAPTER VIII.

It may not be improper here to illustrate the subject, to give some account of the progress of railroad invention, which, like the steam-engine and steamboat, was effected by a succession of inventions and improvements to cheapen labor, and meet the ever-extending demands of trade and commerce.

The first account we have of any attempt towards a railway-track, was made by Master Beaumont, who, as early as 1630, laid down wooden rails to haul his coal from near Newcastle-upon-Tyne to the river. The rails were laid in the ground for the wagon-wheels to run on, and thus overcome the friction produced by the yielding surface of common roads. By the embedding of plank or rails, it was found that one horse would draw a loaded wagon ordinarily requiring two; and that the expense of transporting the coal for shipment was thereby reduced about one half. These were used some forty or fifty years, before the idea of laying parallel rails was entertained; when, in 1676, a track was laid with parallel rails, and the wagon wheels so fitted as to be guided by and run upon them.[1] These roads were in use a hundred years or more, without any essential improvement; were run in the same old way, and were, for aught that appears, confined to the hauling of coal on the banks of the Tyne. The

[1] *Life of George Stephenson*, p. 68.

coal was transported from the mines, a distance varying from three to ten miles.

In 1791, one Benjamin Outram made an improvement upon these roads, by making the upper surface of the wooden rails convex, and applying cast-iron wheels with a concave periphery, so that the wheel and rail closely fitted each other. These roads were called Outram roads, and afterwards, by a contraction of the name, "tram-roads."[1] Before this, as early as 1738, iron rails were used at Whitehaven. We find them also in Scotland, in 1767. In 1776 we have an account that the Duke of Norfolk laid iron rails upon cross timbers, and spiked them to the timbers, for the use of his colliery at Sheffield; and in 1789, one William Jessup built a railway in Leicestershire and used cast-iron edged rails, with flanges upon the tire of his wagons.[2] In 1800, Benjamin Outram used stone in lieu of timbers for supporting his rails; but experience has shown that stone, from its non-elastic character, is not so suitable for cross-ties as timber.

It will be noticed that these "tram-roads" were entirely worked by horses; and various schemes were proposed, meanwhile, by these projectors to save the expense if possible of horse-power. One genius proposed sails as the cheapest and best way of running the "tram-roads;" but he found his motive power so unsteady and fluctuating, that he abandoned the idea of its utility. Steam-power seemed to them, after all, to be the only thing that could be successfully employed

[1] *Westminster Review*, July, 1857, p. 121.
[2] *Life of Stephenson*, p. 70.

as a substitute for animal power. Much speculation had been indulged in by one and another, as to what steam might do if applied to land carriages; but no one could contrive any mode of making the application.

The notions of men differed essentially on the subject, and each one who took the matter into thought seemed to have a theory of his own. One Chapman tried an experiment, by stretching a chain from one end to the other along the centre of his track, with the chain passing once round a grooved barrel wheel, which turned under the centre of the engine, and as the wheel turned the engine moved along slowly;[1] but this proved a tiresome and profitless business. Another man of the name of Bronton, of Derbyshire, rendered himself famous by the invention of what he called his "Mechanical Traveller," for which he took out a patent. It was constructed to travel upon legs, "working alternately like those of a horse." But it blew up in one of his experiments, and killed several persons, and thus the anticipations of the inventor were brought to a sudden close.[2]

It was not discovered until 1813 (then by Mr. Blockett), that smooth wheels would adhere sufficiently to the rails, to draw any number of wagons attached behind; and the absurd idea, that the wheels must be cogged or toothed, was exploded.[3] Before this a track containing four rails was used; two for a set of cog-wheels running on the outside, and two for a set of smooth wheels on the inside, to sustain the weight

[1] *Life of Stephenson*, p. 81.
[2] Lardner *On the Steam-engine*, 7th edition, p. 338.
[3] *Life of Stephenson*, p. 85.

of the load. Stationary engines were proposed and strongly advocated for the transportation of coal and other heavy loads on "tram" ways; but this was found more expensive than horse-power, and given up. Indeed, so strongly was the prejudice fixed in favor of the great utility of "tram-roads" worked by horses, that but few persons could persuade themselves that steam could be used with as much economy or profit as horse-power. Even Tredgold, that distinguished railroad engineer, then supported the opinion that locomotives could not be driven so fast as horses, and that stationary engines, if any were used, would be most economical and safest — and, moreover, that any velocity beyond ten miles per hour, could in no case be expected.[1]

Previous to 1829 no locomotive had exceeded six or eight miles per hour.[2] Even the Killingworth railway, which Stephenson first constructed (in 1814), using the ordinary steam-engine, worked but four miles per hour, and was the most successful of any then constructed; yet it worked clumsily, and was found not to be so economical as horse-power. The prejudice against railways, in the mean time, on account of the competition they created with the laboring classes, was very great; and tended to check improvement in the system. Even up to the time of constructing the Liverpool and Manchester Railway, it met with such opposition on the line of it, among the people, that

1 Tredgold *On Railroads*, 2d edition, p. 119.

2 The Stockton and Darlington Railroad, constructed by George Stephenson, was opened on the 27th of September, 1825; and was the first railroad ever opened for freight and passengers; yet the speed of the engines did not exceed six miles per hour; — a speed that passengers of the present day would hardly have the patience to endure.

they drove off the surveyors with guns, and pitchforks, and other deadly weapons; pelted them with stones and missiles, and insulted them in all manner of ways.[1] Meanwhile political economists were divided on the subject of their utility; some strongly advocating the cause of the laboring classes, and supporting them in their ill-founded belief, that their work, and with it their bread, was in danger of being taken from them.

But no human effort can check the progress of art, any more than it can check the progress of freedom. Both will work their way in spite of opposition, and achieve new triumphs, to a more glorious consummation in the future. Step by step this great work went on, and various were the experiments to construct a railroad track and car in such a way as to adapt them to the old steam-engine of Watt, which engine they seemed to look upon as a fixed thing, admitting of no alteration or improvement. Thus, in the words of the venerable Dr. Cotton, "they sought to fashioneth the house to the hangings, instead of the hangings to the house."

Not so with Read. His great purpose had been to reconstruct the steam-engine, knowing that it could not be successfully applied to locomotion, without very extensive modifications; in short, he had labored to "fashioneth his hangings to his house." To this end, he had invented the multi-tubular boiler, as a substitute for the old one; had dispensed with the condenser; and by his own calculation, which seems not to have entered before into the mind of any one, he applied the steam force of two atmospheres, instead of

[1] *Life of Stephenson*, p. 168.

one, to his piston, and thus converted the condensing engine of Watt into a complete working portable high-pressure engine,—the only engine that can be properly used on railways. The steam-engine, thus modified by him, reached the point of being light and portable. It not only dispensed with the weight of the condenser,[1] but of the water to be used to produce condensation,—the air-pump, working-beam, and other portions of the machinery, as well as the brick work and extra weight of the boilers of the old stationary engines. This was twelve years before the steam-engine was known to be used in the form of a high-pressure engine; and the invention actually produced that change in the use of steam as a locomotive power, that it remained only to be applied, to open that railroad system which has since assumed such vast proportions. Read, though the inventor in 1788, and patentee in 1791, of this high-pressure portable engine, never himself succeeded in securing the necessary means to apply it to practical use; but that part of the work, in obedience to a stern necessity, he was obliged to leave to others to accomplish; and it has been applied by one and another, until it has become the chief motive power, not only for land transport, but for inland navigation to a very great extent, wherever industrial labor, commerce, and civilization have found their way.

[1] Leopold, a German, gave an account, in 1718, of two engines, the invention of which he imputed to Papin. One was like the engine of Savary, the other was an engine in which steam, by means of a four-way cock, and two cylinders and pistons, without the aid of the atmosphere, was made to work the engine without condensation; but it does not appear that any very definite notion was entertained as to the tension of steam required to work it.

Oliver Evans, in 1801, was the first person known to introduce high-pressure steam to practical use, which he applied for grinding plaster and sawing marble, in Philadelphia. Trevethick & Vivian were the next, in 1802, who are known to have used an engine of similar construction[1] which was many years after Read's invention.[2] Neither Evans or Trevethick & Vivian, however, introduced the multi-tubular boiler, but each used a boiler with a single cylinder, with the fire made within it.

"Richard Trevethick, a captain in a Cornish tin-mine, and a pupil of William Murdock, determined to build a steam-carriage, adapted for use on common roads. He took out a patent in 1802, and Andrew Vivian, his cousin, joined him in his patent, Vivian finding the money, and Trevethick the brains. The steam-carriage built by Trevethick presented the appearance of an ordinary stage-coach on four wheels. It had one horizontal cylinder, which, together with the boiler and furnace-box, was placed in the rear of the hind axle, and the motion of the piston was transmitted to a separate crank-axle, from which, through the medium of a spur gear, the axle of the driving wheel (which was mounted with a fly-wheel) derived its motion. It is also worthy of note, that the steam-cocks and the forcing-pump, as also a bellows, which he used for quickening combustion in the furnace, were worked off the same crank-axle; and that the piston was not only raised but depressed by the

1 Woolhouse, vol. i. pp. 41, 141; *Rep. of Arts*, vol. iv. p. 241, New Series; Renwick *On the Steam-engine*, p. 254, *post*.

2 "High-pressure engines usually work with a tension of five to six atmospheres; and may, with proper construction and care, be used with equal safety, as condensing engines; and are far more economical, where the saving of weight, room, and cost is an object; as in case of locomotives, and boats for river navigation." —Renwick, pp. 180, 183.

action of the steam, being in this respect (erroneously says Mr. Smiles) 'an entirely original invention, and of great merit.' This was the first locomotive put into practice. Trevethick & Vivian determined to exhibit their machine in the capital. They set out with the locomotive from near Land's-End, where it was built, for Plymouth, to be conveyed from thence to London on a vessel. Coleridge relates, that while the vehicle was on the way to Plymouth at the top of its speed, it tore away a gentleman's garden fence; and on approaching a toll-gate Vivian called out to Trevethick to slacken speed. He immediately shut off the steam; but the momentum was so great that the carriage came dead upon the right side of the gate, which was quickly opened by the toll-keeper. 'What have we got to pay here,' asked Vivian? The poor toll-man, trembling in every limb, and teeth chattering, essayed a reply. 'Na, na, na, na' — 'What have we got to pay, I say?' 'Na — nothing to pay! My de— dear Mr. Devil, do drive on as fast as you can, — nothing to pay.' The carriage safely reached London and was there exhibited; and it dragged behind it a wheel carriage filled with passengers. It was impossible from the badness of English roads to introduce it into practical use; and after exhibiting it as a curiosity, it was abandoned by Trevethick as a practical failure."[1]

In 1804 Trevethick & Vivian constructed a locomotive, to run on tram-ways, for mining purposes. The first trial it dragged several wagons, carrying about ten tons of iron, five miles per hour. "Yet it proved like the first steam-carriage, a practical failure. It was never employed to do regular work, but was abandoned after a few experiments, as the rails were little calculated to sustain so heavy a weight; and the

1 *Life of Stephenson*, pp. 76, 77, 78.

engine was taken from the wheels and put to work at one of the pumps in the mine.[1] The periphery of the wheels of Trevethick & Vivian's locomotive was made rough by bolt-heads, to keep the wheels from slipping; and afterwards in 1811, racked or toothed wheels and rails were used for the same purpose, by Blenkinsop of Leeds, who for several years transported coal with them from Middletown to Leeds, a distance of three and a half miles, dragging some thirty coal cars, at a speed of three or four miles per hour. These were really the first earnest working experiments of the locomotive used and continued for practical purposes. These engines were worked with two cylinders.[2]

The boiler of the above locomotive of Trevethick & Vivian, was of cast iron, and unsafe; and although it contained but one tube, yet it was in the form of the letter U, passing in a curve through the boiler with one end used for a grate and furnace, and the other connected with the smoke-pipe, to emit the smoke and heated air. The engine had no condenser, and was worked by high-pressure steam; and was used on a tram-road at Merthyr Tydvil in South Wales, to transport heavy materials in mining operations.[3] The same year, 1804, that Trevethick & Vivian tried their engine, Oliver Evans also put an engine of the high-

[1] *Life of Stephenson*, p. 79. [2] *Ibid.* p. 80.

[3] *Cyclopedia of Useful Arts*, p. 324. Mr. Trevethick, in his evidence before a Committee of Parliament in 1831, testified, "that his Merthyr Tydvil engine was a detached ingine, independent of all fixtures, without condensing water, and the fire enclosed in a boiler surrounded by water, and a forced draught to prevent a high chimney; it was independent from brick-work, light, safe from fire, and occupying but little room."

pressure principle into his dredging-machine at Philadelphia.[1] The engine of Evans, however, retained the working-beam, which may be regarded as an advantage in propelling boats, but could not be used in locomotives. It is stated by Professor Renwick, in his treatise upon the steam-engine, "Not the least of the improvements of Evans lies in the form of his boilers, which he was the first to make in the form of a cylinder, — a form preferable to any other yet proposed."[2] As already seen, the boiler invented by Read was in the form of a cylinder, and designed for strength, as well as occupying but little space.

By returning to Judge Read's letter to Mr. Jefferson of the date of January 8, 1791, it will be noticed, that he speaks of two models of boilers he had exhibited to the Commissioners the winter previous; but which he withdrew, and substituted therefor the one on which he received his patent. A sketch of one of the boilers withdrawn is found among his papers, which will show that he, as appears by this drawing and description of it, constructed the model of a boiler, in which the flame and heated air passed through the tubes, and consumed the smoke. A copy of the drawing, and short memoranda upon the same paper, is all that remains of his account of this invention. The paper is filed in his own handwriting, "Steam Boiler 1790," and under the drawing is written, in his handwriting also, —

"Section of a steam-boiler which exposes a large surface; is fed from the top through the large tube *a*, and the hot

[1] Müller's *Physics*, p. 517. American edition.
[2] Renwick *On the Steam-engine*, p. 255.

air and smoke passes up through the winding passages and escapes at *b b*.

"*N. B.* — The boiler constitutes the whole furnace, except the brick work at the bottom; and it consumes the smoke — *o o*, float."

This seems to establish the fact that he invented a tubular boiler of each kind: one with the water passing through the tubes, and the other with the flame consuming the smoke. As seen from the plan, this boiler also was cylindrical. His mode of feeding the furnace with fuel down the large pipe *a*, is a matter for the curious; this large tube *a*, added much to the amount of surface exposed, and served as a part of the fire chamber of the furnace; when closed at the top, as was doubtless proposed, it would cause the flame and heated air to pass through the tubes; and his arrangement under the base of the tube *a*, or fire-chamber, to sustain the fuel by a thick plate of iron, with open grates at each end to admit a current of air, would produce a strong draught through the small tubes, and increase the flame; while the float *o o* would not only indicate the height of the water in the boiler, but work a valve in the pipe that replenished the boiler with water from the reservoir. The water in the reservoir would also be heated before entering the boiler, by the smoke-pipes, and a section of the fire chamber passing through it. As the plan does not exhibit any other part of the machinery, it does not show his mode of conducting the steam to the cylinder and working the engine; which doubtless was designed in the ordinary form. We will now proceed to notice improvements upon the steam-cylinder.

PLATE 3

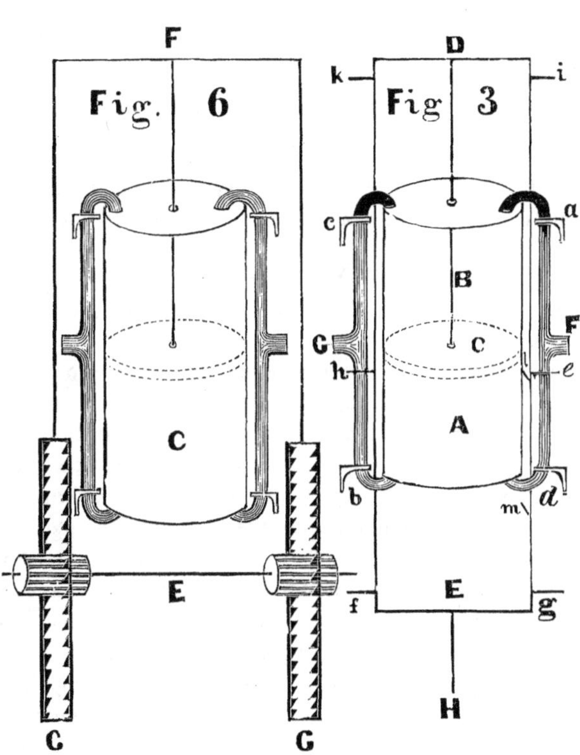

CHAPTER IX.

His improvement upon the steam-cylinder, contained in his patent, will fully appear from the following draught and specification of it, filed with the Commissioner of Patents: —

"Specification of an Improved Steam Cylinder, advantageously constructed to work in an horizontal position.

Plate III.

"Figure 3 is a perspective view of the cylinder and working frame. *A B*, the cylinder which is closed at the end *B* like the common cylinder; the other end, *A*, is also closed by a cap or plate which can be occasionally taken off; *C*, the piston constructed in common form; the stem *D* moves air tight in a collar of hemp, tightly compressed in a stuffing-box that is fixed to the centre of the plate or cap *B*; the working frame *c c* is fixed to the stem of the piston, by which it is moved back and forth; *F*, the steam-pipe coming from the boiler and dividing itself into two branches which enter the ends of the cylinder; *G*, an eduction-pipe leading to the condenser. This pipe is formed by two branches or pipes that convey off the steam alternately from each end of the cylinder; *a b c d*, cocks or regulators. These are alternately opened and shut by the pins *e f g h i k*, in the working frame. As the working frame moves towards *D*, the pin *e* opens the regulator *a*, and lets the steam from the boiler into the end *A* of the cylinder, while the pin *g* closes the regulator *d*, and shuts off the steam from the end

B of the cylinder. Meanwhile the pin *h* closes the regulator *c*, and the pin *f* opens the regulator *b*, and the steam will pass from the end *B* to the condenser, while the end *A* will be replenished from the boiler; in consequence of which the piston will move from *A* towards *B*, and the pins of the working frame will open the regulators that were closed, and shut those that were before opened; then the end *A* of the cylinder will be exhausted, and the end *B* replenished with steam, and the piston will move back with equal force, and the whole operation be again repeated. NOTE, — Sliding-plates or regulators, like those made use of for other engines for letting in and shutting off steam from the cylinder, may be substituted for the cocks or regulators *a b c d*."

The above invention was expressly designed to adapt the steam-engine to land carriages. This was fifteen years before Evans and Trevethick & Vivian tried their first experiments with the locomotive. And although the machinery will not compare in its style with the more elegant and finished machinery of the present day, yet proper allowance will be made for this, as it was the first essay, as is believed, to change the steam-engine to the great purpose of locomotion. Notwithstanding the simplicity of its construction, it embraced the principle, if it did not attain to the more elegant and complex mechanism of our present locomotive engines.

The above cylinder so nearly resembles the cylinder of Trevethick & Vivian, which they first used, it would almost seem that theirs was constructed after Read's plan. The following description of their cylinder will be interesting to the curious on this point: —

"The cylinder was placed upon its side, and in one position of the cock a communication was opened between the boiler and one end of the cylinder, while another communication was opened between the other end of the cylinder and a tube leading to the chimney (or the condenser, as the case might be). Steam was thus admitted to act on one side of the piston, and allowed to escape from the other side to the chimney. When the piston attained the end of the stroke the position of the cock was reversed, and the steam, which had just driven the piston in one direction, was allowed to escape to the chimney, while steam from the boiler was admitted on the other side of the piston, to impel it in the contrary direction; and in this manner the piston was continually driven backward and forward, in a horizontal direction, and parallel to the direction of the load. The piston-rod was moved through a hole, corresponding with it in magnitude, in the cover of the cylinder, in which it was rendered steam-tight by a stuffing-box properly lubricated."[1]

The above description of Trevethick & Vivian's cylinder is a good description of Read's, and indeed, nearly an exact one. It is certainly a matter of interest to know how it happened, that in the first locomotive ever put in operation, for which Trevethick & Vivian have the credit of the invention, the cylinder admits of the same description precisely as that of Read's, which he invented and patented fifteen years before.

The following extract of a letter from Judge Read to the Hon. Timothy Pickering, will throw some further light on this subject: —

"BELFAST, *January* 27, 1817.

"HON. TIMOTHY PICKERING.

"SIR: . . . . On examining my papers at Belfast,

[1] Vide *Cyclopedia of the Useful Arts*, p. 324.

6

I find that it is upwards of twenty-six years since I invented the steam-engine, with horizontal arms, similar in principle to the engine for which Mr. Trevethick has recently received a patent in England. I have now in my possession a drawing of the engine, and an accurate description of its principles, construction, and operation, and of the manner of connecting it with the boiler, copied in the year 1789, from my original draught, by Mr. William Shepard Gray, the cashier of Essex Bank.

"With assurances of my highest respect and esteem,

"N. READ."

The mere idea of applying steam to land carriages, as before stated, was not new. Watt and his journeyman, Murdock, entertained the idea, and, in short, tried to apply their condensing engine to a small model; but they wholly failed in the experiment; and Watt himself said that there was no use in attempting to apply it.[1] And in a letter to Mr. Boulton, September 12, 1786, in referring to Murdock's speculations on the subject, he says: —

"In the mean time, I wish William (meaning William Murdock) could be brought to do as we do, — to mind the business in hand, and let such as Symington and Sadlier throw away their time and money hunting shadows."[2]

He regarded the thing as impracticable, from the great heft of the engine, unless it could be so modified as to make it portable.[3] Read's improvements were designed to reduce the weight of the engine, and make it portable. Hence he styled it the "Portable Steam-engine." Watt did not seem to discover any mode

[1] Muirhead's *Life of Watt*, p. 343, *post*. [2] *Ibid.* p. 349.
[3] *Ibid.* p. 340.

of doing it. He suggested the idea of applying a rotative reacting steam-wheel, of the form of Barker's centrifugal reacting water-wheel; but said of it, "This would not abridge the size of the boiler; and I am not sure that such engines are practicable."[1] Indeed, "the impossibility of using the condensing engine was ascertained and admitted by Watt."[2]

It is claimed for Oliver Evans that he was the first to apply the steam-engine to a locomotive. It will be remembered that his experiment was the same year as that of Trevethick & Vivian, — 1804. They were contemporaries in the construction of their locomotives; but which first "fired up" their engine does not appear, and is not very material for us to consider. Evans did not, however, construct his machine for running upon the land, but on the water; and only proposed to convey it to water from the place of building, — being about a mile and a half from the Schuylkill, at Philadelphia. His machine weighed about twenty-one tons, and he designed it for dredging merely. He put a steam-engine in it for the purpose of working it on the river, and at the same time availed himself of the power of his engine to convey the machine, or mud-scow, to the river. To accomplish this purpose he placed wheels under it, and turned the wheels with the engine, which readily transported his dredge to the water.[3] Trevethick & Vivian's machine was designed to run upon a railroad track, or tram-road, as then called, for the purpose of transportation upon the

1 Muirhead's *Life of Watt* p. 348.
2 Renwick, *On the Steam-Engine*, p. 297.
3 *Lives of Eminent Mechanics*, p. 76.

land. Hence to them is justly given the credit of running the first locomotive, properly so considered.

Prof. Renwick states that "Evans was the first who entertained rational hopes of being able to move carriages by steam;" and "not only was the first to entertain correct views, but was also the first to submit them to practice in the removal of his dredging machine."[1] In view of what has been shown, these conclusions are erroneous in point of fact, and not warranted by any just interpretation of the case; which can be accounted for in no other way than that the professor had not then been informed of what others had done. In the first place, it is difficult to see why he should give the preference to Evans, who had constructed no locomotive with a view to its use upon the land; while Trevethick & Vivian had constructed theirs and applied it expressly for that use. In the second place, this experiment of Evans's was made fifteen years, as before noticed, after Read's invention of the high-pressure steam-engine, and his improvements to adapt it to land carriages, of which he constructed a model. Evans's engine, moreover, though acting upon the high-pressure principle, did not approach so near the locomotive-engine of the present day as Read's. Instead of the multi-tubular boiler, constructed with numerous small tubes passing through it, as now used, his boiler consisted of only one large tube, or flue, passing through its centre.[2] He also retained the old Newcomen working-beam, with his cylinder standing in an upright or vertical position; while Read intro-

[1] Renwick's *Treatise on the Steam-Engine*, p. 297.
[2] Müller's *Physics*, p. 518.

duced the cross-head, and placed his cylinder in a horizontal position. This arrangement of machinery by Evans never has been used for locomotives, and in point of fact is wholly impracticable for such a purpose. Thus with an engine that never has or could be used with success, it must be regarded as a great stretch of credulity to believe that "Evans not only was the first to entertain correct views, but was also the first to submit them to practice."[1]

Evans's experiment was but a rude invention to convey his scow to the river; yet, like many others before him, he doubtless had it in mind to show that he could move a machine upon the land, as well as upon the water, by the force of steam, — an idea he had long entertained, and for which he had been much ridiculed. His machine was simply a large flat, or scow, and his engine of five horse-power, designed for raising the mud into the scow. He made wooden axle-trees of rough timber, of sufficient length for the scow to rest upon, and used wheels constructed like common cart-wheels.[2] He had a wheel inside the scow, which he turned with the engine, and this wheel gave motion to the wheels below, by means of a chain or rope that passed round the hub of this and one of the forward wheels, which was also connected with one of the hind wheels in a like manner.[3] His load was a heavy one

[1] The *Encyclopædia Britannica*, vol. xx. p. 581, 1860, expresses similar views, taken, no doubt, from the above remarks of Prof. Renwick. It says, "To him (Evans) may be attributed the rapid advancement of America in all that relates to the introduction of the steam-engine, in its multifarious applications, and especially in steam navigation." These contagious opinions are apt to be worth but little.

[2] Hows' *Memoirs of American Mechanics*, p. 76. [3] *Ibid.*

for his engine to move on a common road, and it progressed very slow; but he succeeded in conveying it to the river, where the scow was taken from the wheels and launched into the water. This was the only endeavor ever made by Evans to move a land carriage by steam.

Evans, however, is entitled to great credit for his improvements upon the steam-engine; but they were many years subsequent to the inventions of Read, whose engine was not only the first, but a more perfect and complete development, of the high-pressure principle.

The following is a copy of the plan and specification of the steam-carriage invented by Read, which he presented with his petition to Congress for a patent, in 1790: —

"PLATE V.

"Fig. 1. Description of a steam-carriage.

"*A A A A*, the wheels of the carriage. *B B*, the hubs of the hind wheels, extending some way on the ends of the axle-tree in the form of trundles, or pinions, which, with the wheels, are moved round upon the axle-tree by racks with flexible teeth, like those described in Plate III., Fig. 6. *C*, the boiler. *D D*, two pipes constantly conveying steam from the boiler to the cylinders *E E*, which are in a horizontal position. Each pipe divides itself into two branches, which, as in the engine before described, alternately convey steam to each end of the cylinder. *F F*, the working frames. *G G*, the racks with flexible teeth, which constantly turn the wheels round the same way, whether the plunger moves backward or forward. *H H*, the tongue turned back under

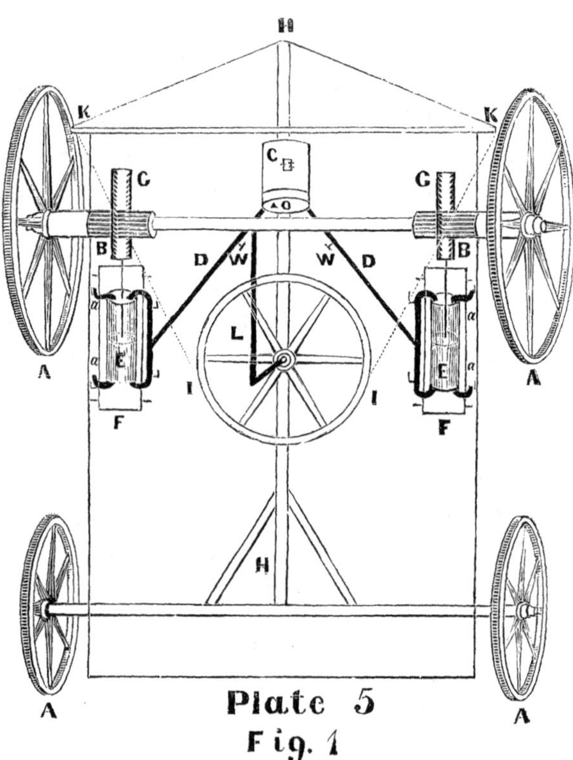

Plate 5
Fig. 1

the body of the carriage. *I I*, a horizontal wheel between the tongue and body of the carriage. *K K*, two pulleys fixed on the hind part of the carriage. *I K*, *I K*, two strong ropes or chains proceeding from opposite sides of the wheel *I I*, and passing over the pulleys *K K*, and then made fast to the end of the tongue *H*. *L*, the director, by which means the wheel *I I*, and consequently the tongue and carriage, are turned one way or the other, as occasion requires. *W W*, two cocks to shut off the communication of steam between the boiler and either or both of the cylinders, as circumstances may dictate. *a a a a*, eduction-pipes, with cocks alternately to convey off the steam from each end of the cylinder. The cylinders are worked without a condenser, by letting the steam vent itself against the atmosphere; in consequence of which it is necessary that the condensation of steam in the cylinders should be equal to the pressure of two atmospheres, in order to produce the same effect it would with a condenser when the condensation was equal to the pressure of one atmosphere. The ends of the short pipes *a a a a* are turned back, that the carriage may have an additional impulse forward.

"The carriage may be turned either way with great facility, by means of the cocks *W W* and the director *L*. To turn the carriage to the right, the right-hand cock *W* should be closed more or less, according to the shortness of the turning, which will check the operation of the right cylinder, and consequently retard the motion of the right wheel, and at the same time tend to accelerate the motion of the left wheel; which prepares the carriage to be turned with ease by moving the director to the left. After the carriage is turned, the steam-pipe should be opened as before. To turn the carriage to the left, a contrary operation is necessary. When you want to stop the carriage, close the steam-pipes *D D*, by turning the cocks *W W*, and the steam in the boiler will vent itself at the valve nigh the bottom of the boiler, without endangering the engine.

"NOTE. — The whole of the machinery for moving and directing the steam-carriage, except the top of the boiler, the director, and two regulating cocks, are, for conveniency, placed under the body of the carriage.

"NOTE. — The cylinders may be placed perpendicularly, and impel the carriage forward by means of clicks and movable pinions; but experience alone will determine the best method."

This steam-carriage, simple in its construction, will, nevertheless, show important facts in relation to Read's improvements, at that early day, upon the steam-engine, to fit it for propelling land carriages. It shows that he proposed to place the cylinders in a horizontal position, and turn the wheels by applying the piston-rod directly to them, without a working-beam; that he dispensed with the condenser, and calculated that the density of steam in the cylinders, on that account, should be equal at least to the pressure of two atmospheres instead of one, — an important fact, as before noticed.[1] This, with the invention of the multi-tubular boiler to raise high steam, changed Watt's condensing into a high-pressure engine complete in all its parts, and dispensed with a large share of the bulk and weight of the engine. Watt, Murdock, Symington, Sadlier, and others had speculated upon the same thing, without being able to make such a change in the steam-engine as to apply it to locomotion; and Watt, as before stated, admitted that the condensing engine could not be used for such a purpose.[2]

[1] *Ante*, p. 72.

[2] The following brief account of Murdock's experiment is quite amusing:

Prior to 1790, when Read petitioned Congress[1] to secure a patent for his invention of land carriages to be driven by steam, no successful application of steam-power had ever been directed to such a purpose except to meet with insurmountable difficulties, and be rejected as a thing impracticable.[2] The idea that it was capable of giving wings to the traveller, and transporting overland, as it now does, the commerce of nations, was at that time wholly new, and to the mass of mankind was looked upon as a matter equally mysterious and visionary. Even the members of Congress, the congregated assemblage of the wisdom and intelligence of the country, were so skeptical on the subject that when Read's petition for a patent for the application of steam to land carriages was read by the clerk of the House, a general smile was excited among the members, — a different look entirely from that now seen, in the earnest debates of Congress on the several projects for opening lines of railway to the Pacific.

"Murdock constructed, in 1784, a diminutive steam locomotive, heated by a spirit lamp, which ran off from him, in a dark evening, down a lane, in Cornwall, where he was trying it, and was mistaken for the devil by the poor clergyman of the parish, who chanced to be returning home that way just as the fiery little object was in its mid-career." — *Westminster Review*, No. 33, p. 121.

[1] This was before the passage of the "Act to promote the Progress of the Useful Arts."

[2] It is stated in the *North American Review*, July No., 1858, "that the first actual model of a locomotive of which there is any written account was made by a Frenchman named Cugnot, who exhibited it to the Marshal de Saxe in 1763. A second one, which he made for the king, is now preserved in the Conservatoire des Arts et Métiers. It was considered too dangerous a monster to be trusted, as when set in motion it rushed forward and knocked down a wall, after which it was shot up." This must have been tried by the old Newcomen engine, probably, as none other is known to have then been in existence.

The petitioner, who was present at the time his application was read by the clerk, felt stung by the indignity of the House, and he withdrew that part of his petition relating to land carriages. He did this after his papers came before the commissioners of patents, to whom the subject was referred by Congress, on the passage of the act organizing that board. After the withdrawal, the commissioners, through their secretary, Mr. Remsen, requested the renewal of his application for his land carriage;[1] but the manner of the reception of this part of his petition to Congress by that body, was a matter with him not easily overcome. He saw that the members looked upon the subject as visionary, which was quite too trying for his sensibility and better knowledge; and he did not renew this part of his petition, notwithstanding the request of the commissioners, whose duty it was to decide upon the merits of the application. He consequently took no patent for moving land carriages by steam.[2]

There does not however appear to be any knowledge or history before this, of any change of the old condensing engine of Watt, into the high-pressure engine that prepared the steam-engine for land carriages or locomotives. Can it be said, that Evans or any one else before this, invented or applied the multi-tubular boiler, the improved cylinder placed in a horizontal position, with the piston worked both ways by a steam force not less than two atmospheres, and with the cross-head and connecting rods, to a land carriage or locomotive? Did Watt discover this machinery, or Murdock

[1] See Mr. Remsen's Letter on p. 111.
[2] See Appendix No. 3.

apply it to his fiery little devil? And the experiments of Evans, and Trevethick & Vivian, with the locomotive had yet many years to wait. In fact, the above-named inventions embrace the essential parts of the machinery of the locomotive engines now in use.

CHAPTER X.

HAVING said thus much in reference to the adaptation of Read's engine to land carriages, we will now return to the steamboat, and pursue his experiments in relation to that subject. After his improvements upon the steam-engine, he constructed a boat of sufficient size to carry a man, with the view of determining the best mode of propulsion. It appeared to him that paddle-wheels were the most natural means, and by proper adjustment to the engine and boat would work with ease, and impart a greater and more steady propelling force to the boat than any other plan. These had never been tried in America nor in Europe, in the form he proposed to apply them. Perrier had utterly condemned them; and the experiments of Hull and Miller, as will be recollected, were upon different plans altogether; the former proposing but one wheel in the stern of the boat, and the latter using but one between the kelsons of his double craft. From the statement of Read,[1] it appears that none of the above experiments had come to his knowledge when he applied paddle-wheels to his boat. The silence of Dr. Franklin on the subject of paddle-wheels, while he proposed the plan of Bournelli for ejecting water from the stern of the boat, and the opinion expressed by the American Academy of Sciences, and other eminent men in Massa-

[1] *Post.*

chusetts, that they believed Read the original inventor of paddle-wheels, as will appear hereafter, would seem to confirm the idea, that neither he nor they had a knowledge of those experiments.

His boat was constructed in 1789; he attached the paddle-wheels to an axis extending across the gunwales of the boat, turned by a crank; and designed to be moved by his high-pressure engine, with the continuous rotative principle of Watt; which he (Watt) had invented and put in operation in factories some four or five years previous. Watt, as before noticed, had applied this motion to his steam-engine to make it available for turning the wheels of mills [1] and factories, without any thought or purpose of applying it to the wheels of a steamboat.[2] By means of the crank worked by hand, Read propelled himself across an arm of the sea (called Porter's River) in Danvers; his boat went with great rapidity and worked to his entire satisfaction. He then satisfied himself by his experiment that paddle-wheels would drive a boat with great ease and speed, when turned by the power of the steam-engine, and controlled by its steady rotative principle. He at once determined to use paddle-wheels as the mode of propelling his boat, and constructed the model of it accordingly with a view to a patent.

Several gentlemen were present and saw the above experiment with the boat, among whom was Rev. John Prince, D. D., of Salem; as the following certificates of Dr. Prince and William Shepard Gray, in their own handwriting, among the papers left by Judge Read, will more fully show. The paper is filed in

1 *Ante*. 2 Muirhead's *Life of Watt*, p. 330.

the handwriting of Read, "Memorandum of William S. Gray and Rev. John Prince." The following is a copy: —

"MEM°. — In the summer of 1788 I went to assist Mr. Nathan Read in keeping his apothecary shop; the following winter and in the summer of 1789, he was much engaged on mechanical and philosophical subjects; particularly in the construction of a steam-engine, whose power might be advantageously applied to the propelling of boats and carriages; and in order to ascertain by experiment the effect that float-wheels would have upon the boat, I very well remember that he had a light boat built by a Mr. Pierce, to which was attached a pair of float-wheels to be moved by hand — the experiment was tried in Porter's River in Danvers. I was not a witness to it, but was told that it succeeded to his fullest expectations. The boat was afterwards brought back and remained for some time in the back part of the shop; why steam was not applied I then did not make inquiries, and soon after leaving his shop for other pursuits, I made no further inquiries about it, but have since understood it was for the want of a sufficient capital to put it in operation.

"W. SHEPARD GRAY."

"SALEM, *December*, 1816."

"I recollect ye above facts stated by Mr. Gray, and remember to have seen Mr. Read row about ye river in ye boat; but could not ascertain ye time when ye boat was made and used. JOHN PRINCE."

Colonel Pickering, of Wenham, Massachusetts, who was Secretary of State under the administration of John Adams, and a friend and acquaintance of Judge Read during his residence in Salem, and supposed to be familiar with his inventions, speaks of his invention of paddle-wheels as original with him, as late as 1817; which will appear from the following letters of introduction to Miers Fisher, Esq., of Philadelphia, and Richard Stockton of New Jersey, given him on the occasion of his going to Washington that year, on business connected with the patent-office: —

"WENHAM (near SALEM), *December* 4, 1817.

"DEAR SIR: — Allow me to introduce to you my much esteemed friend, Nathan Read, Esquire, the ingenious inventor and improver of several useful machines, on account of which he is now on his way to Washington.

"I believe you were engaged as counsel for your friend, Colonel Ogden, in relation to his controversy with the Fultonites, before the Legislature of New Jersey. At any rate, I presume you are acquainted with the merits of the case. Mr. Read was the real inventor of the essential part of Fulton's machinery — the water-wheels as applied to propel boats by steam. Of this he can produce satisfactory evidence, which he will show you if your leisure admits.

"I pray that Mr. Read, as a gentleman of science and distinguished worth, may receive your attentions.

"With very respectful esteem,

"I am your obedient servant,

"TIMOTHY PICKERING."

"RICHARD STOCKTON, Esq."

"WENHAM (near SALEM), *December* 4, 1817.

"DEAR SIR: You will permit me to introduce to you my worthy friend, Nathan Read, Esq., the ingenious inventor and improver of several useful machines, for some of which he has obtained patents, and is now going to Washington for others. Such a man will find a patron in every friend to practical schemes of public utility, and receive your attentions in particular. But what especially made me desirous of your seeing Mr. Read, was the recollection of your zealous patronage (I think I do not mistake) of Mr. Fitch, in his essays to propel boats by steam. Mr. Read will satisfy you that he was the real inventor of the grand and essential parts of Fulton's machinery, as applied to the moving of vessels — the water-wheels; and stated the same in his petition to Congress, in the year 1790, while sitting at New York, where it was publicly known, and where Fulton, I take it, aided by Chancellor Livingston, began his operations with those wheels.

"With great respect and esteem,
"I am your friend,
"T. PICKERING."

"MIERS FISHER, Esq."

Read's experiment with paddle-wheels, taken in connection with his engine, as shown by his plans, drawings, and model which he had constructed, presented a new combination of machinery, which is claimed to be the first combination brought together, that would admit of success in steam navigation; a large portion of which was of his own invention. Indeed, his machinery was identical in all its essential principles with that used at the present day in the smaller class of boats for river navigation, especially upon the western waters; and nearly identical with that used on the first boat Fulton built upon the Hudson in 1807, which has given him so wide a reputation as the reputed inventor of steamboats.

Feeling a strong assurance of success, he had high hopes and anticipations, and looked forward in the ardor of his purpose to the accomplishment of a work that promised so great a revolution. He hoped, moreover, to share in the benefits of his inventions, and thus obtain a compensation for his labors; and he took measures at once to secure a patent for his improvements. His first step was to lay his inventions before the Academy of Arts and Sciences,[1] and obtain the views of that Society in regard to their originality and importance. Both subjects were examined by a Committee of the Society, upon which they made report, and gave him the following certificate thereof, namely, —

"At a meeting of the 'American Academy of Arts and Sciences,' April 1st, 1784, — *Voted,* That Richard Cranch, Esq., Loammi Baldwin, Esq., the Rev. Joseph Willard, and Mr. Caleb Gannett, be a Committee to receive such applications, as may in future be made to the Academy; and after examination had of any piece of machinery, which they shall judge of public utility, and worthy a patent, they are hereby authorized to give such testimonials, in behalf of the Academy, as they may think expedient.

"Copy examined,

"CALEB GANNETT, *Recording Secretary.*"

"We, the above-named Committee, have examined draughts of improvements proposed by Mr. Nathan Read of Salem, in this Commonwealth, in the steam-engine, and its application to the moving of water (boats) and land carriages. By reducing the size of the apparatus, and yet enlarging the evaporating surface, much originality is discovered, and very beneficial effects will in our opinion be secured, exclusive of the saving in the article of fuel. It appears to us that the advantages proposed by a steam-engine will be enjoyed in a greater degree, with less inconvenience and at a smaller expense, on this construction than on any other within our knowledge. The several plans, we think,

[1] This was before he was chosen a member of the Society.

discover great attention and sagacity in the author; and justly entitle him to the patronage of the Government of the United States; to which, with deference, we recommend him and his improvements, wishing, that in virtue of a patent, he may be enabled to render his theories of public utility, and receive a reward for his laudable industry in the field of science.

"RICHARD CRANCH,
JOSEPH WILLARD,
CALEB GANNETT,
LOAMMI BALDWIN.

"*Commonwealth of Massachusetts,*
BOSTON, *January* 15, 1790."

In addition to the above he also obtained the following testimonial, from the distinguished men of Boston and vicinity, whose names are attached thereto, some of whom were residents of Salem and neighbors of Read; among whom will be noticed the name of John Prince, D. D., the venerable pastor of Salem, who afterwards, in his advanced age, gave the certificate, as before seen, of the experiment with the boat and paddle-wheels: —

"We, the subscribers, having examined Mr. Nathan Read's plans and drawings, designed as improvements of several machines, are of opinion that they are real improvements, and as far as we know are original inventions.

"The portable steam-engine, being so constructed as to work both upward and downward with equal power, appears to be a great improvement, and is capable of being applied to many useful purposes, such as moving boats, wheel carriages, etc.; but this seems to be but a small part of its merit; its portability, from its small weight and bulk, its large evaporating surface, and its being so constructed as to produce large quantities of steam in proportion to the fuel employed, make it superior in those respects to any other we are acquainted with.

"E. A. HOLYOKE,
JOHN PRINCE,
JOHN WARREN,
COTTON TUFFTS,
B. LINCOLN,
A. DEXTER,
E. WIGGLESWORTH,
JAMES WINTHROP,
SAMUEL WEBBER,
ELIPHALET PEARSON,
NATHANIEL W. APPLETON.

"SALEM, *January* 20, 1790."

Congress at this time was in session in the city of New York. With the above testimonials, his plans and drawings, and the models of his steamboat and land carriage, he went to New York, and on the 8th of February, 1790, — about two months before the passage of the "Act to promote the Progress of the Useful Arts," — presented a petition to Congress for a patent. The following is a copy of his petition, so far as it relates to the subject under consideration : [1] —

"*To the Honorable Congress of the United States:* The petition of Nathan Read of Salem, in Massachusetts, respectfully showeth ; . . . . that he has also invented a portable steam-engine, which may be constructed with less expense, is much lighter, occupies less space, and requires far less fuel, than any other within his knowledge. Your petitioner has likewise discovered an improved method of applying the

[1] The same petition contained other applications not connected with steam; and having no relation to the subject, that part of the petition is not copied.

power of steam to the purposes of navigation; and has formed a plan to facilitate land carriage by the same agent. The machinery for communicating motion to boats, vessels, land carriages, etc., is very simple, and takes up but little room.[1]

"The models, draughts, and descriptions of the above-mentioned machines, engines, etc., having been critically examined, and the principles on which they are constructed fully approved as just and philosophical, by a select committee of the American Academy of Arts and Sciences, and by several other gentlemen, eminent for their skill in mechanics and every branch of physics, your petitioner is induced from the extraordinary expense, which in a young country always attends first essays of every kind, to solicit such aid from this honorable body as will enable him to bring into general use such machines, engines, etc., as may be judged worthy of particular encouragement, in consequence of their subserviency to other arts and manufactures, and their direct tendency to facilitate the inland trade and navigation of the country, as well as to enhance the value of the Western Territory, by having the effect of diminishing its distance from the seat of government. Your petitioner also prays, that the benefits of his inventions and improvements may be secured to him, his heirs, and assigns, for such term of years as Congress may think fit.

"NATHAN READ.

"NEW YORK, *February* 8, 1790."

He spent most of the winter of 1789–90 in New York, and exhibited the plans, drawings, and models of his boat, and also of his steam-carriage, to President Washington (to whom he had letters of introduction from General Benjamin Lincoln), and also to members of Congress and other gentlemen there; among whom

[1] See his Specification, *post*.

were several distinguished mechanics, and explained to them the principles of his machinery.[1]

While in New York he boarded at Mrs. Wheaton's, in company with Dr. Cutler and General Rufus Putnam, who were attending upon Congress as the agents of the Ohio Land Company. They introduced to him John Stevens of Hoboken, who called upon them at their quarters. At this time, Read explained to Stevens, who took a deep interest in the subject, the principles of his "multi-tubular boiler," and its adaptation to boats and land carriages; and in the mean time exhibited to him the plans and drawings of his boat with paddle-wheels, and his mode of turning them by his improved cylinder, etc.[2] Stevens at that time had become interested in steamboat projects, which was probably unknown to Read. He had appeared before the New York legislature as the competitor of Rumsey on his application, before that body, for his water-ejecting steamboat, pipe boiler, and raising water for mills; and in conjunction with Rumsey, in opposition to the law which Fitch had previously obtained, for building steamboats in that State.[3] And this same winter that he examined Read's plans and drawings he left the New York legislature (followed by Rumsey and Fitch), and presented his petition to Congress for a patent for generating steam and for propelling vessels by steam. It is probable that the examination of Read's plans and drawings, and his models (for it seems he had his models with him), gave Stevens a new impulse in his steamboat projects.

1 See Judge Read's letters to Timothy Pickering and D. Read, *post.*

2 Letters of Judge Read, *post.*

3 See page 128, *post.*

Read's steamboat was designed to be moved by the "multi-tubular boiler" he had invented, his improved cylinder, acting under Watt's double-action principle, and paddle-wheels; and his engine carried by high steam, to be used with or without a condenser. This properly fitted it for river navigation with boats of small size; river navigation being then the sole purpose in view. The following is a copy of his description of the boat, or specification connected with the drawings: —

"Description of a boat or vessel to be impelled through the water and against the stream of rapid rivers, with great velocity, by means of float-wheels moved by the steam-engine.

A. The hulk of the boat or vessel. (See Plate III. Fig. 5.)

B. The Portable Boiler, in the bottom of the boat.

C. The new constructed cylinder, firmly fixed at such distance above the boiler, as to admit the axis of the float-wheels to turn freely and to be raised or lowered as occasion requires.

D D. The float-wheels, the floats of which should be large in proportion to the size of the boat, and the velocity with which it is to be moved.

E E. Pinions fixed on the axis of the float-wheels.

F. The working frame, which should move in grooves to keep it steady and in its proper place.

G G. Two racks on each arm of the working frame, each of which has a set of flexible teeth alternately moving the pinion the same way. One rack or set of teeth turns the pinion as the plunger descends, and the other rack on the opposite side towards the pinion the same way when the plunger ascends; in consequence of which the float-wheels

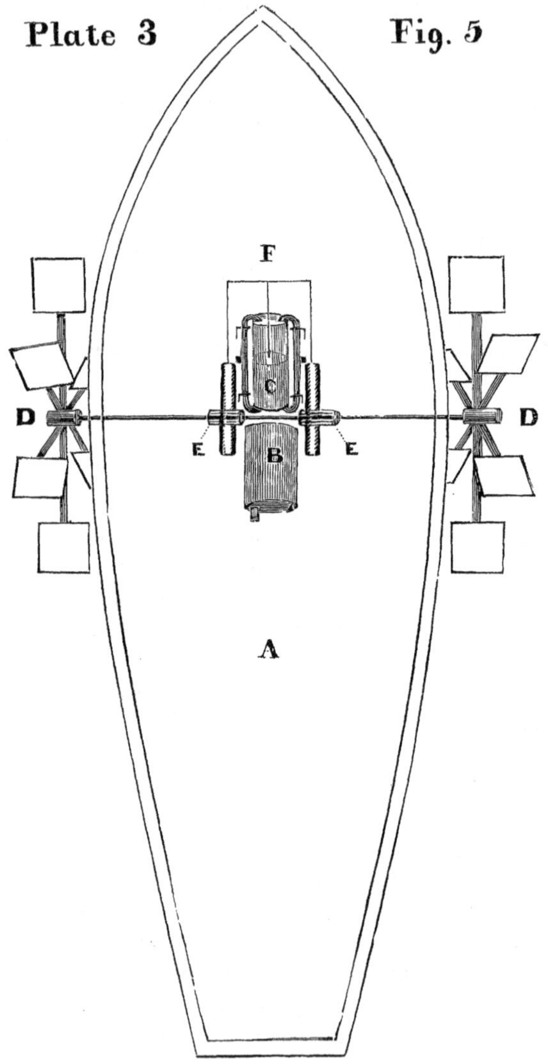

Plate 3 Fig. 5

have a continually progressive motion. The flexible teeth in the racks are so formed as always by their own gravity to keep their proper places, and be ready to act. A continually progressive motion may also be given to the boat by means of two movable wheels and clicks, which alternately move the pinion on the axis of the float-wheels, and constantly turn it the same way. Either method in practice is very simple, and the work contained within a very small space. There may be a small forcing-pump to convey the water reproduced from steam in the condenser directly back into the reservoir, which is much more economical than to supply it with cold water."

The Congress of 1789–90, being the first after the close of the laborious and stormy work of establishing the Constitution of the United States, was as yet but imperfectly organized. It was moreover crowded with business of the most important and exciting character; and had but little time or thought to bestow upon applications of a private nature. In the mean time no patent laws or regulations had been established or patent granted by the General Government. Soon after his petition was presented to Congress the "Act to promote the Progress of the Useful Arts" was passed, constituting the Secretary of State, Secretary of War, and Attorney General, a board of commissioners, to whom all matters of this character were to be referred; and his application thereupon came before the Commissioners. He first asked for a patent for a boat consisting of paddle-wheels, his newly invented boiler, and improved cylinder, and for land carriages driven by steam.[1] But unluckily for the petitioner, in looking

[1] *Ante.*

over some of the old volumes of the "Transactions of the Royal Society," he chanced to notice an article, relating to an experiment a long time previous, in France, in which it was related, that paddle-wheels and oars both had been tried, to see if they would not control the action of a ship of war in a calm, which experiment before that had never come to his knowledge.[1]

Erroneously supposing that such experiment interfered with his right to a patent for a boat with paddle-wheels, he withdrew so much of his petition as related to them; and under date of January 1, 1791, presented a new petition, and substituted a new propelling agent, which he denominated a "rowing machine," which he had invented and constructed upon the principle of the chain-pump, working in a horizontal position, parallel to the keel of the vessel, with one half of the chain and paddles under water and the other half out. This, he believed, would answer the next best purpose to paddle-wheels; but he reluctantly made the change, as he considered the paddle-wheels the preferable mode.[2] But laboring under the impressions stated, and feeling bound to obey the provisions of the law, that seemed to require something wholly new and never before thought of, he took a patent for a boat to be propelled by the rowing machine, for his portable furnace boiler and improved cylinder, as shown by the patent heretofore inserted.[3]

1 See letters to Timothy Pickering and D. Read, *post*.

2 *Post*.

3 Extract from Specification: "The rowing machine will revolve like the chain-pump, and the paddles on the lower half of the chain will be continually passing from head to stern in a direction parallel to the keel,

It can hardly be doubted, even at the present day, but that the chain-wheel may be applied with tolerable success to boats for river navigation; yet that it is equal to the simple paddle-wheel for river or ocean navigation, is not to be allowed; this sufficiently appears from the adoption and general use of the latter. Such, indeed, was the opinion of Read, and he was entitled to a patent for paddle-wheels; certainly as much as Fulton was, when he (Fulton) received his patent for them in 1811, twenty years after. And it is but just to allow to Read, as much for his original and avowed purpose of using them, as if he had actually patented them; they formed a part of his original steamboat.

If the above view of the case be correct, it follows that Read's true combination of machinery for his steamboat, consisted of Watt's double-acting principle, with his own tubular boiler, improved cylinder, and paddle-wheels; a combination of machinery that essentially makes up the inland steamers of the present day.[1] We may be the more justified in looking at the

broadside against the water, and impel the vessel forward, while the paddles on the other half of the chain pass back from stern to head, out of water, without resistance. This motion by a crank may also be given. The size of the machine should be increased or diminished, according to the power applied and the resistance to be overcome."

[1] The multi-tubular boiler is used at this day in many English boats. Its tubes are placed in a vertical position, and the water instead of the flame passes through them. The tubes are used in the same way as in Read's boiler but shorter. The drawing may be found in the *Encyclopædia Britannica*, vol. xx. p. 651, which remarks, — "There are three kinds of marine boilers in use in this country, namely, the rectangular flue boiler (which is now very generally discarded), the multi-tubular boiler, or as it is more usually called, the tubular boiler, and the shut-flue boiler. The tubular is that in most general use, in which a large heating surface is crowded into a very small space, and the form of the tubes affords great strength. Shut-

subject in the above light, as we consider how much bulk and weight he had dispensed with in his improvements; the furnace and boiler, instead of occupying two separate positions, were now reduced greatly in size and occupied but one position, while the power was increased; the condenser might be dispensed with also, or retained if desired; a large share of the expense of fuel was provided against; and although his plan of a boat shows the application of the double rack and pinion for turning the wheels, yet in his specification of the chain-wheel, the idea of applying cranks, if found on trial to be preferable, is secured. But the racks and pinions having flexible teeth, worked as well backward as forward, and would produce a continuous rotary motion to the wheels as well as a crank. But experience has shown that the crank is the preferable mode; yet either may be worked by the double-acting engine.

The paddle-wheel had been rejected by Fitch, and also by Perrier, partly on account of the oblique resistance it met with, as the paddles entered and emerged from the water;[1] which difficulty would be greatly increased as the boat was laden; as the wheels would thereby be deeper immersed and become useless. Read had anticipated this difficulty, and to obviate it, as may be seen from his description of his boat, he so constructed them as to be raised or lowered as occasion might require. In giving the rotary motion to his

flue boilers are constructed with numerous flats, with spaces between them, alternating with water and flame, from one and a half to two inches apart. These are more durable against oxydation from salt water, and were used in the vessels of the Peninsular and Oriental Companies."

1 *Ante.*

engine, it would seem that he proposed the rack and pinion or crank, as desired, though his draught is after the former mode. Both were contained in his specification on which he secured his patent, and it will be recollected that he used a crank to turn the wheels of his boat when he made his first experiment with it at Danvers. At this day, now that cranks have become so familiar from their use, the idea of using the rack and pinion would be regarded as somewhat crude; but as he considered either of them practicable, it seemed to be his purpose to secure both, and leave it for future experience to determine their comparative utility.

The invention of a continuous rotary motion was no modern thing; whether it had its origin in Egypt, Arabia, or China, no one knows; but it had been in use ever since the invention of the potter's wheel, or of the common turning lathe; which are moved by the foot by means of a treadle united to a crank by a connecting-rod. The old fashioned spinning-wheel, used for twisting the thread of the flax, as drawn from the distaff with the thumb and finger, is a machine of the same sort; yet strange as it may seem, when cranks had been in such long use for these purposes, and in constant operation for ages before the eyes of the world, no one, until about 1780,[1] conceived the idea that they could be applied to any other possible use than to turn the simple machines above named. Pickard, about 1780, happened to think of applying them to a horizontal shaft to be moved by steam;[2] and the idea of making the steam-engine turn a crank, was about the same time also conceived by Watt, and put in oper-

[1] *Life of Watt*, p. 180; Irving's *History of the Steam-engine.* [2] *Ibid.*

ation by him, in the Albion Mills, which was in 1787,[1] only the year previous to Read's improvements of the steam-engine. No fly-wheel was required for his carriage or paddle-wheel boat, to carry the motion beyond the dead points of the piston, as the wheels themselves were all that was required to perform that service. Of course he would make no representation of a fly-wheel in his plans.

[1] *Ante.*

CHAPTER XI.

THE name of John Stevens, of Hoboken, has been mentioned in connection with his steamboat projects. He was then a man of extensive wealth[1] and great perseverance, and the father of John C. Stevens and Robert L. Stevens, who since that day have distinguished themselves so much in steam navigation upon the Hudson.

Stevens seems to have become somewhat enthusiastic on the subject of steamboats,[2] and, backed up by his extensive means and partiality for mechanical pursuits, he resolved to try his fortune in the attempt to build one. He, as before noticed, soon after his examination of Read's drawings and model, petitioned Congress himself for a patent for generating steam and for propelling vessels by steam. Thus his petition and Read's became pending before the House of Representatives at the same time. This called the attention of Congress to the subject of patents, and it was referred, on the 8th of February, 1790, to a special committee, consisting of Messrs. Burke, Huntington, and Cadwallader.[3]

The result of these petitions was that the committee reported to the House the bill "to promote the Prog-

[1] Renwick, p. 283. [2] *Life of Fitch*, p. 383.

[3] *Journal of the House of Representatives*, p. 30, A. D. 1790.

ress of the Useful Arts," which was passed on the 10th of April following.

In due time the Board of Commissioners, consisting of Thomas Jefferson, John Knox, and Edmund Randolph, was organized under the act. Fitch, however, was displeased with some of the provisions of the act, and had no great liking for Mr. Jefferson. He hence resolved to petition Congress directly, instead of the Board of Commissioners, asking for an independent law granting to him the exclusive right of propelling boats by steam in the waters of the United States, which Congress refused. This petition was dated July 1, 1790, and some five months after Read and Stevens had made their applications to Congress. Fitch being now turned over to the provisions of the general law, along with the rest, afterwards, on the 22d of November, 1790, sent in his petition directly to the Board.[1] Rumsey also had a petition pending before them, presented by his agent, he then being in England.

Rumsey's petition was for a boat propelled by ejecting water at the stern; Fitch's for propelling with oars or paddles, and by forcing water or air through a trunk; Read's for his multi-tubular boiler, improved cylinder, and for a boat with paddle-wheels; and Stevens for propelling vessels by steam, and for a new mode of generating steam.[2] It may be well here to notice, that the history of the respective cases precludes the idea that any of the other petitioners could have derived their inventions from Stevens; while, on the other hand, the claims of Stevens, and the propriety

[1] *Ante.* [2] *Post.*

or justice of his petition for a patent for propelling vessels by steam, and for a new mode of generating steam, as the original inventor, was questioned. During these proceedings, Read had noticed the experiment in France with paddle-wheels, as before stated.[1] His business before Congress had been brought before the Commissioners, after the passage of the act, by two new petitions direct to the Board, — one presented April 16, 1790, for his improvements upon the steam-engine, and the other April 23, 1790, for his method of moving land carriages by steam, and propelling boats or vessels by the same agency by paddle-wheels, etc.[2] To simplify the business, he withdrew both of the above petitions, and presented his petition of January 1, 1791, in lieu of them. In his last one he left out his land carriage, and substituted the chain-wheel for paddle-wheels. After thus arranging his papers, Mr. Remsen, the Secretary of the Board, wrote him as follows, as the Committee had been expected to meet in February : —

"PHILADELPHIA, *January* 25, 1791.

"SIR :— The Commissioners named in the 'Act for the Promotion of Useful Arts,' judging it most expedient not to proceed further in the business thereby committed to them, until a Bill supplementary to said Act, and which is now before Congress, passes, have directed me to inform you, that the hearing of the parties who have applied for patents for the discovery of new applications of steam to useful purposes, cannot take place on the first Monday in February, which was the time they had assigned for the purpose ; but

1 *Ante.*

2 See his draught and description of his steamboat, before given, *Ante.*

that they will be duly informed of the day as soon as it is fixed.

"I am, sir, your most obedient

"Most humble servant,

"HENRY REMSEN, Jun.[1]

"Mr. NATHAN REED."

Previous, however, to the above letter, Read had written to Mr. Jefferson, inclosing to him his petition of January 1, 1791, and in this letter says: —

"Having improved some of the machines for which last winter I solicited a patent, and desirous after further improvement, and communicating others to the public, I must request your Excellency to solicit the Honorable Board to grant me leave to withdraw my former petitions, paying all charges that have arisen, and to present the inclosed petition, in which I have stated, agreeable to the order of the Honorable Board, the nature and extent of the discoveries therein mentioned. . . . . I have requested Mr. Remsen, by permission of the Honorable Board, to inclose me my former petitions, and to deliver to my order several models, which have too long incumbered your office."

The above new petition does not differ from those previously presented, except in the changes before mentioned; and its terms are fully shown by the several specifications, heretofore noticed and filed in the Patent Office on the issuing of the patent.

On returning the old petitions Mr. Remsen writes as follows: —

"PHILADELPHIA, *February* 5, 1791.

"SIR: —You will receive, herewith inclosed, the petitions you presented to the Board on the 16th and 23d of April

[1] This letter has the frank of Mr. Jefferson upon it.

last.[1] The models referred to in them were removed from New York with the effects of the office, and will be delivered to any person empowered by you to receive them. They suffered no injury by the removal, having been carefully packed with paper shavings in a box provided for the purpose. I have concluded to hand this to Mr. Goodhue for transmission, as his franking it will save the postage that would accrue on its being sent without a frank, and as its going by that conveyance is certainly safer than by stage. You will excuse me for observing, that your last petition substituted for the two now returned, does not include as many objects as they do. Your application for a machine for moving and directing land carriages by steam, is not therein renewed, although it should have been if you still persist in it. I should have retained the petition No. 2, had you not inserted in the last one sent your improved method of impelling boats or vessels through water, because it contained your claims for these two objects. You may however draw it over again, leaving out what is included between the brackets, and send it as soon as you please.

"I am, sir, with due respect,

"Your most obedient servant,

"HENRY REMSEN, Jun'r.

"MR. NATHAN READ."

We may now look upon these several projectors prosecuting their claims before the Commissioners for a common purpose — the invention of the steamboat; and each one aiming to secure letters-patent from the government, granting exclusive privileges in steam navigation, according to the several plans they presented. At that time, the great work of applying steam to navigation in the United States was concen-

[1] For these petitions, see Appendix, No. 4.

trated in the efforts of these men. Miller had abandoned his experiments, and all was quiet in Europe on the subject, and Fulton was at work as a journeyman painter in the studio of West in London ; and the idea of engaging in any steamboat project, was as foreign from his mind as the Atlantic Telegraph, and sixteen or eighteen years had yet to pass before his first boat would appear upon the waters of the Hudson.

It is now a conceded point, that American enterprise and genius produced the steamboat ; and it may be well to look at this point of time, and this nucleus of projectors, to determine how large a proportion of that enterprise and genius is due to them ? And here again, a just discrimination should be made between these men, to see who among them had done the most to change and fit the steam-engine for the work. Rumsey had tried his brief experiments upon the Potomac ; but had done nothing to improve the steam-engine and prepare it for navigation. Fitch, with indomitable perseverance, had succeeded in driving his boat six or eight miles per hour ; and by constant repairs run it for some time at a daily loss. Did he reach the secret of success ; and wherein did he leave the steam-engine any better fitted for navigation, than when he found it? Stevens had sought to acquire a knowledge of steam force from such sources as suited his convenience, and took this occasion to place a petition by the side of the others for a patent. The Commissioners met on the 4th of April, 1791, and agair on the 22d and 23d of the same month. After thes meetings of the Commissioners, Mr. Remsen agair writes to Read as follows : —

"PHILADELPHIA, *July* 1, 1791.

"SIR: — I received your letter of the 18th of May last a few days since.[1] The Commissioners, at their meeting in April, agreed to grant patents to all the claimants of steam-patents, so far as they had applied steam to useful purposes, without taking it upon themselves to ascertain whether those claimants were really the inventors, as they severally alleged in their petitions. Accordingly John Fitch for applying steam to navigation; James Rumsey for generating steam, applying it to navigation, and to raise water; yourself, (and) John Stevens for generating steam, applying it to raise water, to work a bellows, and to propel a vessel; and Engleback Cruise to apply steam to raise water, are all to have patents. But neither these or any other patents have as yet issued, owing to the absence of the President, who will sign them, and two of the Commissioners. I presume they will all be finished ready for delivery by the last of this or beginning of the next month, till which time no certain opinion can be formed as to the amount of the fees each patentee will have to pay. By a late order of the Commissioners you will have a patent for your applications of steam which will come to — including the expenses to which the patentees are subjected by law for their petitions and specifications — about five dollars. I return you the models you first lodged, being twelve pieces in the whole, and if you find among them any not belonging to you, I must request the favor of your sending them back. These models are the only ones I am not perfectly acquainted with; they were deposited in Mr. Alden's time, and consisting of many pieces, got mixed with other models, in the removal from New York. I also return your specifications that you may execute them in the customary form, and you may put them under cover to Mr. Jefferson when executed. You will be so good as to men-

[1] No copy of this letter is found among Judge Read's papers.

tion to him whether the models,[1] which Captain Needham will deliver to you, are the same you lodged with the Commissioners in New York. When the patents are made out, I will let you know it.

"I am, sir, with respect,

"Your most ob't humble servant,

"HENRY REMSEN, Jun'r.

"NATHAN READ, Esq."

Patents were afterwards issued to each of the above claimants, under date of August 26, 1791, according to their respective applications, on the principles indicated in the above letter of Mr. Remsen. These were the first patents ever issued under the authority of the United States. Read's was for his portable furnace-boiler, constructed internally with seventy-eight small tubes, and his improved cylinder;[2] and to each of the petitioners, himself included, for applying steam to navigation by such modes of propulsion as they respectively claimed in their petitions, leaving it for the patentees to settle the controversy between themselves whenever their patents should be found to clash with each other. Were we allowed to question the judgment and justice of such men as Thomas Jefferson, Henry Knox, and Edmund Randolph, who constituted the Board of Commissioners, we might say that this was not only a novel, but unjustifiable procedure. The duty of this very Board was to settle and decide upon the respective claims that came before them, and not turn over the parties to the

[1] It is much to be regretted that these models have not been preserved. They are not among the effects left by Judge Read at his residence; nor did he leave any memorandum showing what became of them.

[2] See his patent, specification, and drawings, *ante*.

adjustment of their rights by a wholesale system of litigation, more intolerable perhaps than a voluntary surrender of those rights. It does not appear, however, that any litigation grew out of this dilemma between these patentees; but this was owing more to the incredulity of the public in their steam projects, and the consequent discouragement they met with at that early day in the prosecution of their labors, than to the position in which the Commissioners left them. I deem it proper, however, to notice that none of the other patents granted on that occasion came in collision with Read's;[1] neither of the other parties claimed the portable furnace, *alias* multi-tubular boiler, improved cylinder, or chain-wheels. But the claims of Fitch, Rumsey, and Stevens clashed in several respects.

Fitch's patent was, —

"For applying the force of steam to trunk or trunks, for drawing water in at the bow of a boat or vessel, and forcing the same out at the stern, in order to propel a boat or vessel through the water. For forcing a column of air through a trunk or trunks, filled with water by the force of steam. For forcing a column of air through a trunk or trunks, out at the stern, with the bow valves closed, by the force of steam; and for applying the force of steam to cranks and paddles for propelling a boat or vessel through the water."[2]

Rumsey's patent was, —

"For propelling boats or vessels by means of the reaction of a stream of water, forced by the agency of steam

1 See Read's patent and specifications, *ante*, p. 48.

2 Westcott's *Life of Fitch*, p. 327.

through a trunk or cylinder, parallel to the keel, out at the stern; and for a more ample and easy mode of generating steam, by passing a small quantity of water through an incurvated tube ⌗ placed in a furnace, whereby the action of fire is communicated to the water and steam in all its passage from the entrance to the exit, and which kind of boiler can be easily adapted to every species of fire or steam-engine; and for raising water by steam for the turning of mills, or for agricultural or other purposes." [1]

Stevens's patent did not differ essentially from Rumsey's, being for generating steam with a like boiler, and propelling his boat in a like way; by forcing water through a trunk by steam and ejecting it at the stern of the vessel; and also for raising water for mills, etc., and working a bellows.[2] It will thus be seen that the patents of Rumsey, Fitch, and Stevens, clash in several particulars; but that neither of them interferes with the patent of Read.

1 This description is taken from Rumsey's specification of his steam inventions as presented by him to the New York Legislature, and is supposed to be the same as that he soon after presented to Congress. —*Documentary History of New York*, vol. ii. p. 1099.

2 See Report of Committee of New York Legislature, on the Petitions of James Rumsey, John Stevens, and John Fitch, in 1789.—*Ibid.* p. 1092.

CHAPTER XII.

There is an item in this history that should not be passed over here. In December, 1788, James Rumsey petitioned the Legislature of New York for a grant for propelling boats by forcing water through a trunk, for his pipe-boiler, and for raising water for mills, etc., by steam; and on the 9th of January, 1789, John Stevens (*alias* John Stevens, Jr., as then called) also presented his petition to the Legislature of New York, for a grant similar to that applied for by Rumsey. Fitch, who had obtained a previous grant from the legislature, remonstrated against these petitions; and the subject having been referred to a special committee, consisting of Messrs. Livingston, Havens, and Van Cortland, they reported: —

"That nothing in the act, securing to John Fitch the exclusive right of propelling boats by fire or steam, can be construed to prevent the legislature from securing to James Rumsey, for a limited time, the exclusive right of generating steam, by his new invented method of a pipe-boiler; and further, that they have examined the petition of John Stevens, and the draughts accompanying the same, and are of opinion, that the method proposed by him for propelling boats by steam, does not materially differ in its principles from the mode proposed by James Rumsey, and that he stands in the same situation with respect to John Fitch as the said James Rumsey."

The Committee reported a bill to secure to Rumsey his pipe-boiler, and rejected the petition of Stevens; Rumsey's bill, however, was not passed by the New York Legislature, and Fitch's rights in that State remained undisturbed.[1]

The above proceedings before the Legislature of New York, show several important facts, namely, that the controversy between Fitch, Rumsey, and Stevens, commenced in the New York Legislature, in an attempt there made by Rumsey to supplant Fitch, and overturn the rights he had acquired under his act, and of Stevens to supplant them both, in an effort to secure a grant, which Fitch and Rumsey contended did not belong to him, either by invention or priority; that the applications of Rumsey and Stevens were substantially for the same thing; each having a like mode of generating steam, propelling boats or vessels, and raising water for mills, etc.; that the pipe-boiler, so much talked about, consisted of one single incurvated pipe, holding about three gallons of water, twisted about in a brick furnace, and giving no opportunity for steam to escape from it but at one end, while the other end received the water from the reservoir.[2] From these facts we are enabled to distinguish between their pipe-boiler and Read's multi-tubular boiler; and, moreover, to learn that Read incidentally met these three contestants before the Board of Commissioners, free from any concert or collision with them;

1 *Documentary History of New York*, vol. ii. p. 1092.

2 See specification of James Rumsey, *Documentary History of New York*, vol. ii. p. 1099, and affidavits of Charles Morrow, p. 1027, and Joseph Barnes, p. 1028.

and that Rumsey and Stevens, after trying their case before the New York Legislature without disturbing the rights of Fitch there, removed their controversy, and sought to obtain from the General Government what they could not get from the State of New York.

To show that Read's patent was clear of any interference from the others, we need only make the proper distinction between the pipe-boiler, patented to Rumsey and Stevens, and the multi-tubular boiler, patented to Read. This distinction may, to a considerable extent, be at once seen by looking at the diagrams of the pipe-boiler and furnace, on the opposite sheet, and comparing them with the drawings of Read's multi-tubular boiler and furnace.[1] But to see how entirely unlike they are, we are not only to look at the form of their construction, but at the more important difference there is in their power and capacity for generating steam, and in their strength, durability, and safety. The following is Rumsey's description of the pipe-boiler, now in the possession of the American Philosophical Society, in his own words :[2] —

"A B C, an iron pipe bent as represented by the figure; D F, a pipe of the same size with the valve E, on the turned-up end. The end F, is brazed to the boiler A B C, at B, and hangs down in a perpendicular direction to discharge the steam at the valve E, when the machine is not at work. This boiler is set up in a furnace of brick, and the fuel put into the cavities formed by the crossings of the pipe. The water that makes the steam is forced in at the end A, by a small pump. The advantage of this boiler is, that it presents a much greater surface to a small fire

[1] *Ante*. [2] See No. 11, on opposite sheet.

than any other. The furnace is two feet square inside; one hundred and twenty feet of pipe, two inches in diameter, is bent as represented in the diagram, the surface of which will be sixty feet square,[1] all of which will be in the fire, as the fuel is to be burnt in the cave made by the crossing of the pipe, and must therefore be very hot." [2]

From the above description and diagrams of Rumsey, and the specification and drawings of Read,[3] we are led to a full discovery of the dissimilarity of the two boilers. The eye can determine the difference in the form, and no comments on that subject are required, as they are at once seen to have little or no resemblance to each other in this respect. We will then proceed to inquire in general terms into their power and capacity for generating steam.

The pipe-boiler exposes sixty square feet of surface to the fire, and but one single aperture of the size of the interior diameter of the pipe, for the steam to escape from, at the extreme end of the pipe where it is connected with the cylinder. The multitubular boiler (invented to be longer or shorter at pleasure), allowing it to be but six feet in length, and the average length of the tubes but five feet, there being seventy-eight tubes proposed in the drawing, would expose one hundred and ninety-five square feet of surface to the fire, and have seventy-eight apertures for the steam to escape from. This makes one aperture to every two-and a half feet of surface exposed to the fire, the same the pipe-boiler had for

[1] He means sixty square feet, as is shown by the length and diameter of the pipe.

[2] Westcott's *Life of Fitch*, p. 228.

[3] *Ante*, p. 50.

sixty feet. In short the pipe-boiler had but one of these apertures, while the multi-tubular boiler had seventy-eight of the same size. It will moreover be seen, that the multi-tubular boiler ejects the steam from the upper end of each of these seventy-eight tubes, into an apartment at the top of the boiler, where the steam is compressed, and from whence, as the cocks are alternately opened and closed, it rushes through a steam-pipe of sufficient size and capacity to conduct it to the cylinder; while the steam from the pipe-boiler is conducted directly to the cylinder, without an opportunity to acquire force from compression. This would reduce the power of the pipe-boiler even below the comparative amount of steam it was capable of producing; but the amount of steam it produced, when compared with the multi-tubular boiler, may be readily seen by the most inexperienced eye.

How much better would a pipe be one hundred and twenty feet in length, resting in a furnace in a series of incurvations, within a space of two feet square, and exposing sixty feet of surface to the fire, than one but twenty feet in length, of the same size, and exposing but ten feet of surface to the fire? This is a question that can be answered only by a series of experiments with exactness; but it is self-evident, that a pipe one hundred and twenty or but twenty feet in length, and only two inches in diameter, exposed in the manner described to the intense heat of a furnace, would, either of them, generate as much steam as could pass out at one end. If such be the case, a pipe one hundred and twenty feet in length is no better than one of but twenty. But here is another matter to be considered: in a hot furnace the water would occupy but the first part of the pipe, and the steam the other part, and it becomes an inquiry of some importance, what effect the heat of the furnace would have upon the steam as it passed through one hundred feet of pipe intensely heated? If it could not find vent and wholly escape from the end of the pipe, the pipe itself must explode; and oxydation would soon destroy it, if not destroyed by the expansive force of the steam.

There could, moreover, be neither strength, durability, or safety, in the pipe-boiler. However well it might be constructed, the heat of the furnace, as well as the expansive force of the steam and oxydation, would destroy it; and if the heat should be raised very high, it would at once fuse that part of it unoccupied by water. Fitch was persuaded to try it once, against his opinion of its utility, and then it exploded, and he flung it aside. Rumsey had the utmost faith in it, although "it kept melting off his solder and coming to pieces." At best, its power was limited to very light work; and it was wholly worthless for navigation, or any use where the ordinary power of steam was required.

The multi-tubular boiler, on the other hand, is capable of exerting the highest degree of steam-power, not only for driving mills and factories, but for propelling vessels of the largest class,[1] — every part of it

[1] "The *Great Eastern* is supplied with three distinct modes of propulsion — paddle-wheels, screw-propellers, and sails. The engines for driving the paddle-wheels are horizontal, of which there are four; they are of one thousand nominal horse-power each, with four cylinders 74 inches diameter, and length of stroke 14 feet, with 15 revolutions per minute. Each

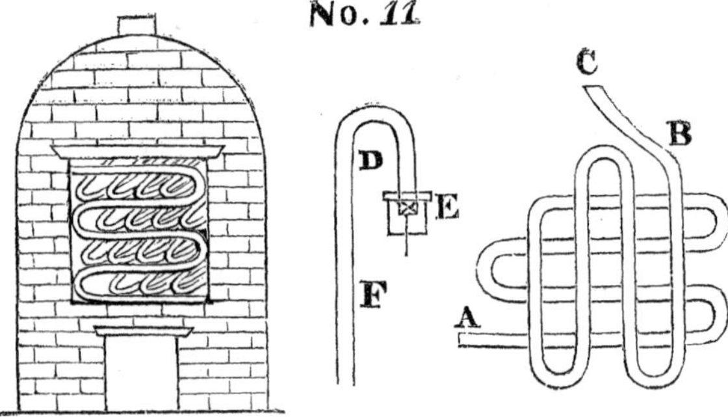
No. 11
C
B
D
E
F
A

comes in contact with the water, is free from oxydation, less liable to explode, and infinitely more efficient in the generation of steam. In fact, it has so little resemblance to the pipe-boiler, not only in its form and manner of construction, but in its durability, power, and fitness, as to bear no comparison.

It has been imputed to Stevens that he was the inventor of the multi-tubular boiler.[1] We have no evidence that he ever claimed it himself; his petitions to the New York Legislature and to Congress, and his patent, do not show it; but the report of the Committee of the New York Legislature, that his and Rumsey's application was substantially for the same thing, each having the same mode of generat-

engine may be worked independent of the others, and combined, work up to 3,000 horse-power, with 15 lbs. of steam; and with 25 lbs. of steam, to 5,000 horse-power. The steam for these engines is generated in 4 multi-tubular boilers, each 17 feet 9 inches long, 17 feet 6 inches wide, and 13 feet 9 inches high, weighing 50 tons and containing 40 tons of water. The tubes are of brass, 3 inches in diameter, and 400 in number; and there are ten furnaces to each boiler. There are 4 horizontal engines, also, for turning the screw-propeller, with 4 cylinders of 84 inches each in diameter, with 4 feet stroke, and 50 revolutions per minute, and working up from 4,500 to 6,500 horse-power. The boilers are 18 feet 6 inches long, 17 feet 6 inches wide, and 14 feet high, six in number, each weighing 57 tons, and containing 45 tons of water. They are multi-tubular, each of them containing 420 brass tubes, of three inches diameter. These boilers may all be applied to either set of engines. There are also two auxiliary engines, high-pressure, of 70 horse-power each, used for lifting the screw and doing other work about the ship, and ten donkey-engines to supply the large boilers with water. The paddle-wheels are 56 feet in diameter, with 30 floats to each wheel, 13 feet in length and 3 feet in width. The screw-propeller is 24 feet in diameter, and weighs 36 tons. It has 4 fans fitting into a large boss on the shaft; the screw shaft is 160 feet long, and weighs 60 tons; it is constructed of iron, forged and put together in sections, the largest section weighing 35 tons." — *Semi-Weekly Courier & Inquirer*, June 30, 1860.

[1] Renwick *On the Steam-engine*, p. 283.

ing steam and propelling their boats, virtually disproves it. In one form and another, all three of the men, Fitch, Rumsey, and Stevens, made their claims upon the pipe-boiler; but it nowhere appears either of them made any claim to the multi-tubular boiler, which was a thing as distinctly marked and as different in principle and construction, almost, as is a lead pipe from a locomotive engine. Indeed, at that day, the multi-tubular boiler had never come into the idea of either of them until exhibited by Read.

If Stevens, or his successors, used the multi-tubular boiler in any of the boats they afterwards built, it must have been many years after Read's exhibition and patent of it. Moreover, the application of Read was pending before the Commissioners, and his patent granted under the eyes of Stevens, and must have been with his knowledge; and if he used it in preference to his pipe-boiler, it would be no more than the use of Read's chain-wheel, which he put into his first boat in lieu of his own water-ejecting mode of propulsion.[1] But it would be no strange thing, if — in the lack of knowledge and discrimination which must needs have obscured the public mind at that day as to the true character of these inventions — the different modes of generating steam, patented at the same time should be confounded, and the two boilers indiscriminately spoken of and imputed to Stevens; more especially as he was afterwards the active man before the world, in the attempt to construct a steamboat, — being previous to Fulton's experiment upon the Hudson, and covering the time when Livingston, Stevens,

[1] See *post*.

and Rosevelt, were in company in their efforts to build a living boat.

It is stated that Stevens used a tubular boiler and a propeller in an experimental boat built at his shop, under the charge of his son, Colonel John C. Stevens, in 1804.[1] This may be true; yet it is no proof that he invented either the one or the other; but the fact that he used it may be an additional reason to show why the invention was imputed to him. If Stevens used a tubular boiler at that time, it would be about the time, or soon after Read's patent of it had expired; and whether the boiler which he used was the multi-tubular boiler patented by Read, or his own pipe-boiler, to which the name of tubular boiler has been sometimes given, does not appear. Professor Renwick in his "Treatise on the Steam-engine,"[2] says: —

> "John Stevens of Hoboken commenced his experiments in steam navigation in 1791. . . . . Stevens's experiments were conducted at intervals up to 1807. During these experiments he invented the tubular boiler," etc.

The Professor makes no distinction here between the multi-tubular boiler and pipe-boiler, but seems not to have understood the difference, or else to have supposed that they meant one and the same thing.[3]

1 See Lecture of Charles King, LL. D., delivered before the Mechanics' Society, New York, 1851.

2 See *post*.

3 Professor Renwick's Treatise was published in 1830, and in his Preface he gives credit to Robert L. Stevens (son of John Stevens), and expresses his obligations to him for the facts furnished by him for his Treatise, in relation to the first steamboats upon the Hudson. Of course the information he received was, on this particular subject, as indefinite as he penned it. Under the idea that the pipe-boiler was the first tubular boiler invented, it would be very natural for Robert L. Stevens to give the credit to his father

Moreover, if it is meant that Stevens invented the multi-tubular boiler "during these experiments," *i. e.* from 1791 to 1807, it could not have been contained in his patent of August 26, 1791, as it was issued upon his application made to Congress, a year or two before he commenced any experiments; and the idea that he invented it during this time is met by Read's previous patent of it, — a fact authenticated in the Patent-office Department, and known to Stevens.

For ten years after Read obtained his patent the elder Stevens was for the most part at work at his shop in Hoboken, trying to build a steam-engine, and sought to raise up mechanics and acquire the needful information for the work; and he built no boat before 1801 of sufficient capacity and completeness to try any satisfactory experiments. This was the one he, Livingston, and Rosevelt commenced together, and which was left on his hands, as will be hereafter seen, when Livingston left the concern and went to France. This boat was so constructed as to be propelled by a "system of paddles resembling a horizontal chain-pump." The invention of this "system of paddles," Professor Renwick[1] also ascribes to Stevens, when in fact it was contained in Read's patent alone. This error can be accounted for on no other view of it than that applied to the tubular boiler. Stevens must have borrowed both of them from Read's specifications and drawings, and after so long and quiet a lapse of time, applied them to his boat, and thus obtained the reputa-

in general terms; and be put down by the writer in terms equally general.

[1] Renwick, *Treatise on the Steam-engine*, p. 284.

tion of their inventor. Stevens himself, however, understood the whole subject, and made no claim to their invention; and it may be regarded as a compliment to Read that Stevens should place such confidence in his inventions, as to try them in the first boat he built in preference to those of his own patent.

As to the "system of paddles," it would be quite natural for any one to suppose that the patentee, to say the least, regarded it as the preferable mode of propelling boats; and this may explain in some measure why Stevens at first constructed his boat with this apparatus attached, and why he also attached the tubular boiler. It will also be seen that Stevens himself, as well as others, finally adopted the paddle-wheel, which Read applied for in his first petition.[1]

[1] One Samuel Morey, of New London, built a small craft in 1793 with a wheel in the stern, something like Hull's. Morey afterwards, by the aid of Burgess Allison, built a boat near Bordentown, N. J., in 1797, with paddle-wheels at the sides: "The shaft moved across the boat with a shackle-bar, commonly so called, which moved on the principle which is now (1819) used in the largest boats." — Duer's *Second Letter to Colden.*

CHAPTER XIII.

But these inventions of Read had a broader application and use than hitherto considered. When Fulton brought himself to the work of practically effecting the great purpose of navigation by steam, — a work which has given to him a name immortal in the annals of his country and of the world, — it will be found on an impartial comparison, that the machinery which he brought together to secure his success was substantially the same, and having the same combination, as the machinery which Read had invented and put together, for a like purpose twenty years before. And it will require no stretch of credulity for any one to believe, when the subject is more fully presented, that Read's plan of a steamboat came to the knowledge of Fulton, and was by him adopted in the construction of his experimental boat upon the Seine, and of his first boat upon the Hudson, which proved to be the first successful steamer ever put in working operation.

The originality of the steamboat, now that it has taken so distinguished a part in the wide field of human enterprise, has been a question that has entered into the controversial claims of individuals and nations. Various persons have appeared before the public and claimed the honor of original inventors of it; and different nations have sought to secure that honor as a source of national pride and glory. Indeed, a vast amount of ink and paper, and laborious research have been expended, in the advocacy and investigation of one man's claim and then another. Meanwhile, legislative bodies have been invoked; laws have been passed recognizing, and thus attempting to legalize fictitious claims; courts and juries have been appealed to for the same purpose; and public sentiment tampered with by one device and another. And yet the question, "Who was the inventor of the steamboat?" has never been settled.

The reason for all this is obvious. It never can be settled so long as there is a purpose to attach the invention to any one man. Lay selfishness aside, and allow to each projector, who had actually contributed more or less toward the work, his equitable share in its honors, according to the aid he gave it and the progress he effected, and there would be no trouble in settling the question. This mode of settlement is just; but it still remains to be made; and let it be done, as time and opportunity and a more intelligent public sentiment on the subject may demand. It is enough for the purpose of these few pages to lay before the public the simple facts, showing the part one individual took in this invention.

I speak of the *invention;* there is quite a difference between the invention of the machinery and the appliance of the necessary means to put that machinery to its designed work. The one is the work of genius, the other of money and mechanical skill; genius works out the invention and gives the formula descriptive of it, while the mechanic takes up the formula and with proper aid puts the invention to its designed use. Should the honor of the invention be transferred to the mechanic because he was the first to put the machinery to practical use? Such was substantially the case of Fulton in his building the first successful steamboat. He really invented no essential part of it, but skillfully put together the inventions of others. He had the means placed at his command, or he could not even have done this. He had nothing to discourage, but everything to encourage him. Fortune, power, and influence, stood at his right hand ready to back him up and sustain him. He was employed by Livingston, the possessor of all these facilities, and a knowledge of the inventions of others to carry out a scheme of great magnitude for their own joint profit and aggrandizement. Were it not for this the first successful steamboat might not yet have been completed, and Fulton, —

> "In life's low vale remote had pined alone,
> Then dropt into the grave unpitied and unknown."

Robert Fulton, who stands so prominent in the history of steam navigation, was born in Little Britain, Lancaster County, Pennsylvania, in 1765. His parents were of Irish descent; his father, who emigrated from Ireland, was in low circumstances, and gave but small opportunity to his children. He died in 1768, when his son Robert was but three years of age, who under the good endeavors of his mother acquired a fair common-school education. He had a taste for study, and a mind ever active in the pursuit of some favorite project; and was in fact, the builder of his own qualifications for the work he pursued at different periods of his life, — a matter so common and so highly commendable among the youth of our country. His early predominant passion was for drawing and mechanics; and at the age of seventeen, he went to Philadelphia, and engaged in painting portraits and landscape views, from which he earned a fair support, and acquired a small amount of property. He resided here until he was twenty-one years of age (1786), and then went with his mother to Washington County, Pennsylvania, where he purchased a small farm for her as a home. The same year he went to England, and engaged in the office of West, the great American artist, as a journeyman painter, where he remained for several years.

After leaving West, he spent two years in Devonshire occupied as a painter. After this, he resided a year and a half in Birmingham, where he first acquired some practical knowledge of mechanics, and obtained, in 1794, a patent in England for a double inclined plane to be used for transportation; and about the same time made an improvement in mills for grinding plaster and sawing marble; also in machinery for spinning flax and making ropes, and constructed a machine for excavating canals.

In 1796 he published a work on canal navigation, in which he proposed the use of the inclined plane to pass boats over ravines and elevated points. He now for the first time set himself up as a civil engineer, and relinquished his profession as a painter. The next year, 1797, he is found in France, making efforts to introduce his canal system there; but soon turned his attention to the purpose of inventing a submarine machine for blowing up vessels of war. He was at work at this invention, under the patronage of the French government, until 1801, during which year he went through with a course of experiments in the harbor of Brest, with his machine, or explosive submarine battery; but not succeeding in destroying any of the enemy's vessels (the English) then blockading the harbor, the government of France withdrew its patronage from him; and being without any employment there, he resolved to leave France and return to England. Before doing this, however, Robert R. Livingston arrived as Ambassador from the United States to the Consular Government of France, and Fulton being a countryman of his, and possessing views adapted in some measure to the enterprising schemes of Livingston, they soon met and made an acquaintance.

Previous to the arrival of Mr. Livingston in France, which was in 1801, it does not appear that Mr. Fulton had given the subject of steam navigation any special attention, farther than what had entered into the thoughts of other mechanics and speculative men of the day, — a mere topic of thought and talk. In a letter to Lord Stanhope, who was interesting himself somewhat on the subject, in 1793, he speaks of steam navigation; but what he said to Lord Stanhope does not appear, as the letter has never been published. He also visited Symington's boat, which the latter constructed for Lord Dundas upon the Forth and Clyde Canal, in 1804; but this was long after his acquaintance with Mr. Livingston, and after he had tried his experiments at Paris, and ordered his engine.

Livingston says, at Paris: —

"He communicated to Mr. Fulton the importance of

steamboats to their common country; informed him of what had been attempted in America, and of his resolution to resume the pursuit on his return; and advised him to turn his attention to the subject."[1]

This shows that Fulton had not given his thoughts to the subject before that time (1801) with any serious intent, which was twelve years after Read had completed his inventions, and tried his boat with paddle-wheels at Danvers.

Chancellor Livingston, who was an eminent statesman and civilian, also took a conspicuous part in the introduction of steam navigation. And before we proceed to a consideration of the experiments made by Fulton under his patronage, we will take a concise view of what Livingston himself had done before meeting with Fulton at Paris. Livingston laid no claims to invention or inventive genius himself, but he possessed that enthusiastic spirit on the subject of steam navigation, which was liable to be awakened by the belief, that it would become a source of great wealth to whomsoever should successfully put it in operation, and succeed in securing its exclusive use and emolument. Ocean navigation was not contemplated; and in order to make river navigation a source of private wealth — of such gigantic proportions as had entered into the mind of this enterprising millionaire, — a monopoly over the inland navigation of the country became necessary as a part of the plan he had in view, for carrying out the grand purpose that lay before him.

He was liberal with his means; and in this instance believed their application promised great public advan-

[1] Colden's *Life of Fulton*, p. 148.

tage, as well as liberal returns for his capital. He, moreover, was a distinguished jurist, and well understood the advantages to be derived from chartered rights, concentrated in a single individual, to the exclusion of a common and public use; but it seems that he then did not fully comprehend the powers that lay between a State and the General Government over the navigable waters of the country.

Livingston made his first essay in 1797, and in connection with Mr. Nesbit, engaged in the construction of a boat upon the Hudson River. They employed Brunel — who became distinguished as the inventor of the block-machine, and the builder of the Thames Tunnel — to take the charge of the mechanical construction of the boat. Livingston in the mean time, having full confidence of success, applied to the Legislature of New York for an act giving him the exclusive right to navigate the waters of New York with boats propelled by fire and steam. To accomplish that end it became necessary to remove Fitch's previous grant, obtained for the same purpose. He therefore petitioned the legislature to repeal Fitch's act under the pretense that Fitch "was either dead or had withdrawn from the State, without having made any attempt, in the space of more than ten years, for executing the plan for which he had so obtained an exclusive privilege, whereby," it alleges, "the same had been justly forfeited."[1]

The legislature, upon these representations, in March, 1798, repealed the act of Fitch, and transferred to Livingston, for twenty years, the rights it covered,

[1] *New York Review*, No. 7, p. 149.

provided "he should within twelve months give proof of having built a boat of at least twenty tons' capacity, to be propelled by steam, the mean of whose progress through the water with and against the ordinary current of the Hudson River, should not be less than four miles an hour; and that he should at no time omit for the space of one year to have a boat of such construction plying between the cities of New York and Albany." [1]

The boat Livingston and Nesbit constructed did not meet the conditions of the law and was abandoned,[2] as the boat was unable to move at a speed beyond about two and a half miles an hour, consequently the act became forfeited; but Livingston procured a revival of it for a further trial. Stevens, as has been noticed, was all this time trying experiments with a view to the construction of a boat, directing his attention, however, for the most part to the workmanship and manufacture of machinery for the purpose, but had as yet not succeeded in building one. To unite their efforts, and bring together a stronger force in the work, Livingston and Stevens and Nicholas J. Rosevelt, entered into a copartnership in 1800, to pursue the object jointly, and commenced a boat. Their proceedings, however, were interrupted and the partnership broken up, by the appointment soon after of Livingston as Minister to France; but Stevens pursued his experiments alone at Hoboken, completed the boat before mentioned, which he tried with the chain-wheel invented by Read; and Livingston "carried to Europe high-raised expec-

1 *New York Review*, No. 7, p. 150. 2 Colden's *Life of Fulton*, p. 146.

tations of success."[1] Professor Renwick, in speaking of their propelling apparatus, says: —

"Their apparatus was a system of paddles resembling a horizontal chain-pump, and set in motion by an engine of Watt's construction. We now know that such a plan, if inferior to paddle-wheels, might answer the purpose; it however failed in consequence of the weakness of the vessel, which changed its figure and dislocated parts of the engine."

From the above, it appears that they followed the plan of propulsion Read had patented, precisely; and with it Livingston went to Europe with his high expectations of success; taking with him a full knowledge of this, and doubtless of the other inventions of Read also.

Rosevelt, after the dissolution of the partnership on the occasion of Livingston's mission to France, acted independent of both Livingston and Stevens, and turned his attention to the Ohio and Mississippi, as the field of his steamboat operations. In 1811 he built the first steamboat on those waters, and in her passage from Pittsburg to New Orleans she had a most wonderful experience and escape.[2]

[1] Renwick, p. 284.

[2] For an account of this adventurous passage, see Appendix, No. 2.

CHAPTER XIV.

We will now return to the experiments of Livingston and Fulton in France. Livingston having besought Fulton to turn his attention to steam navigation, it was arranged that Fulton should enter upon a series of experiments on the subject.

"Fulton suggested that it would not do to trust to the mere ingenuity or theoretic skill of either of them, but that it was indispensable that experiments should be carefully made, upon all the methods of any promise which had been proposed up to that time, or which had occurred to Livingston or himself."[1]

He first went into a course of mathematical calculations to determine the resistance of water, the force to be applied to bodies moving through it, the best form of a vessel for easy movement, "and upon the different means of propelling vessels which had been previously attempted."[2]

He applied his mathematics to paddles, oars, setting-poles, duck's-feet, pump and trunk for drawing in and ejecting water, paddle-wheels, and system of paddles resembling a horizontal chain-pump; he without trial rejected all as impracticable, except the two last;[3] and it is singular enough, that he, first of all, favored the use of the last — the system of paddles resembling a

[1] *New York Review*, p. 100. [2] *Ibid.*

[3] Colden's *Life of Fulton*, pp. 153, 154.

horizontal chain-pump, — which was patented by Read, and which was applied to the boat that Livingston had just before left in progress of construction in New York.

Having decided upon trying this, as he then thought the preferable mode of propulsion, he constructed a small boat, in 1802, and tried his first experiment at Plombieres, where he was temporarily residing. After trying his boat, he wrote to Mr. Livingston at Paris, giving him a minute account of his experiment with his system of paddles or chain-wheel, "and assured him of the certainty of success which they afforded him."[1] Mr. Colden treats this mode of propulsion as if it were an original invention of Fulton; and in relation to the subject he adds: —

"The ingenuity of the little working models which he employed on this occasion, the simplicity of his contrivances, his calculations and demonstrations, are all evidence of his genius, his science, and his practical knowledge. Among the manuscripts he has left are diagrams, drawings, calculations, and notes, which fully explain everything connected with this course of interesting experiments. It would be greatly to be regretted, not only in regard to his fame, but as respects the arts, if they should not be given to the world in proper form."[2]

It is truly to be regretted, that the arts have not as yet been benefited by a publication of these diagrams and drawings; but Fulton's fame has not been injured in consequence, for by comparing them with the diagrams and drawings of Read, their analogy would at once appear.

[1] Colden's *Life of Fulton*, p. 155. [2] *Ibid.* pp. 155, 156.

After the above experiments at Plombieres, it was decided to give a trial to paddle-wheels. In the winter following he applied them to a small working model, tried various experiments, and renewed his calculations respecting them; after which Fulton, in a letter to his friend, remarks, "by very exact experiments I have proved that the wheel is superior to the chaplet," [1] *i. e.* resisting boards with endless chain. Thereupon they determined to construct a boat of some size (eight feet wide and sixty-six feet in length) for experiment upon the Seine, and to apply paddle-wheels as the mode of propulsion. This boat was completed in the spring of 1803, but owing to an accident by which it became necessary to repair the hull, it was not tried until August following. It was then tried in the presence of the members of the French National Institute, who were invited to be present, and of a great concourse of people who assembled to witness the experiment.

The experiments with this boat showed satisfactorily that paddle-wheels were preferable to any other mode of propulsion; and although the boat was not so fast in its movements as had been hoped, it was evident that the same machinery, if of more perfect finish, would greatly facilitate its motion; and it became a safe calculation to allow, that a working-boat constructed after the plan and model of this, would prove reliable and successful for the purposes of steam navigation. Indeed, they looked upon the subject with such confidence that Livingston entered into proposals to Fulton, to join him in the construction of boats upon the Hudson River; which he then did.

[1] Colden's *Life of Fulton*, p. 158.

Thereupon Fulton, August 6, 1803, wrote to Boulton & Watt of Birmingham, "ordering certain parts of a steam-engine to be made for him and sent to America."[1] And Livingston wrote home to his friends in New York, to procure an act, extending to him and Fulton together, for the term of twenty years, the same rights which had been granted to him by the act of 1798, but which had now become forfeited. The legislature allowed the application, and an act was accordingly passed, by which the exclusive right of navigating the waters of New York was granted to Livingston and Fulton jointly.[2]

Before Fulton returned to the United States, he visited the shop of Boulton & Watt at Birmingham, in 1804, and furnished them with plans and drawings of those several parts of the engine which he had, on the 6th of August, 1803, ordered them to furnish; and gave them directions respecting them. He ordered only those parts which would be required to construct an engine of a peculiar kind; and it will be seen, that his order followed the essential parts of Read's machinery, which so modified the engine of Watt as to render it light and portable.

In the letters which Fulton had previously written to Boulton & Watt, "he made inquiries as to the employment of high degrees of heat in small engines, and the limit to which it might be carried in order to render them light and compact."[3] He then explained

1 Colden's *Life of Fulton*, p. 165.

2 This grant to Livingston & Fulton was not made on the ground that they were the inventors of the steamboat; but on the ground merely "that they were the possessors of a mode of propelling boats by steam upon new and advantageous principles." — *New York Review*, No. 7, p. 150.

3 *Life of Watt*, p. 333.

to them that his object in ordering the sort of machinery he had, was to reduce the heft of the steam-engine as much as possible, for the purpose of applying it to a boat to run on the rivers in America. He says, "The only thing which is wanting is to arrange the engine as light and compact as possible."[1] And in a postscript to one of his letters, he speaks of engines which had been proposed to him by Mr. Livingston.

Fulton's visit to England in 1804, was, however, but partially induced by his intention of procuring machinery for his steam-engine, — this was but a secondary purpose with him; and although he had tried his steamboat experiments in France at the solicitation of Mr. Livingston, his great theme, and study, and purpose, was to invent his torpedo submarine boat for destroying vessels of war. The patronage of the government of France having been withdrawn from him, he still pursued his purpose in this matter, and made overtures to the British government, proposing to grant to them the benefit of his invention or project. The British minister made an arrangement with Mr. Fulton to secure his infernal machine and services, more to deprive France of them, and to keep them from threatening their own vessels, than from any expectation or belief that they would be of any importance otherwise. It was on this account that Fulton proceeded to London in May, 1804.

The policy of the British government — being herself then mistress of the seas, and having more vessels of war afloat than all other nations united — was to suppress his machine instead of using it. Hence they

[1] *Life of Watt*, p. 334.

constantly baffled him in his attempts to test the effects of it, and took occasion, as far as lay within the scope of ostensible fairness, to make it appear that the machine was a visionary affair. Most of his experiments thus turned out to be failures; he remained in England and kept at work, without any success or encouragement except his pay (and that for the last part withheld), for two years or more. In October, 1805, however, he succeeded in blowing up a Danish brig of two hundred tons, which had been provided for the experiment, and which was anchored in Walmar Roads, near the residence of Mr. Pitt. The torpedo on this occasion contained one hundred and seventy pounds of powder; and in fifteen minutes from the time of starting the machinery and throwing the torpedo into the water, the explosion took place. "It lifted the brig almost entire, and broke her completely in two. The ends sunk immediately, and in one minute nothing was to be seen of her but floating fragments. In fact her annihilation was complete."[1]

The above matter is related not only to show that Fulton remained in England for some time, even after his engine had been sent over by Boulton & Watt to New York, but that his mind was more engrossed by his torpedo war, than by his steamboat. And such in fact was the case with him not only in Europe but in America after his return; making it, notwithstanding his boat, the prominent purpose before him here. Failing to accomplish his desired purpose in England, and worn out by a long and much neglected series of experiments with his explosive machine, his pay finally

[1] Colden's *Life of Fulton*, p. 59.

all withheld, and everything ending in dissappointment and disgust, he at length returned to New York, where he arrived on the 13th of December, 1806.[1]

Within a few weeks after his return to the United States, he applied to our government to assist him in prosecuting his experiments with his torpedoes. Some assistance was rendered, and experiments tried at Governor's Island; and in July, 1807, — being but a few weeks before his steamboat took her first trip up the Hudson, — he blew up a large vessel, in the harbor of New York, "which had been provided for the purpose."[2] Indeed, he continued these experiments with great earnestness, but without any great success, more or less, up to 1810, when, under the prospect of a rupture with Great Britain, he renewed his application to the General Government for aid in the matter; "and soon after this published his work entitled 'Torpedo War; or, Submarine Explosions.'"[3]

The government, under the prospect of war, extended additional aid to Mr. Fulton, and experiments were made upon an enlarged scale. The sloop-of-war *Argus*, under the direction of Commodore Rogers, was placed in a posture of defense against the torpedoes; and in spite of the attacks of Fulton, successfully defended herself against any injury from his boasted instruments of destruction. The Committee appointed by Congress to examine the experiments and make report, reported unfavorably upon the project as a

[1] This same year, Mr. Fulton was married to Miss Harriet Livingston, a relative of the Chancellor.

[2] Colden's *Life of Fulton*, p. 76.

[3] *Ibid.* p. 83.

means of defense; and Commodore Rogers gave his opinion "entirely against Mr. Fulton's system; and he concludes that every part of it would be found wholly impracticable." It is due, however, to Mr. Fulton to say that Mr. Livingston and Mr. Colden (the latter his attorney and subsequent biographer), who were of the Committee, reported favorably. The report of the Committee, *i. e.* the majority, being against the utility of the plan, as a matter not worthy the further attention of the government, his hope of introducing this favorite scheme of his became vain; yet his mind was occupied with the subject during his life.

CHAPTER XV.

On Fulton's return to the city of New York from England, he also, in connection with his torpedo war, commenced his steamboat. Stevens, having failed in his former experiments, and now learning that Livingston, his former partner, had associated himself with Fulton for the purpose of putting a boat upon the Hudson, resolved not to be outdone; and although the infirmities of age, and the expenditure of a good share of his fortune, had come over him during his protracted experiments, he now renewed his energies, and simultaneously with Fulton, commenced the construction of another boat. And indeed it was but a few days after Fulton made his first trip to Albany, before Stevens also had *his* boat in operation.[1] It may be well here to notice that Col. John C. Stevens and Robert L. Stevens, the sons of John Stevens, now took the active lead in their father's business, and prosecuted the design which he had so long sought for in vain, — a successful steam navigation. And with the experience of the father to teach them how to escape from past errors, and the youthful energies and mechanical skill they possessed themselves, to give a fresh impulse to the subject, they commenced the construction of the *Phœnix*, which afterwards became

[1] *New York Review*, No. 5, p. 103.

so distinguished in the early history of steam navigation. It was built with paddle-wheels at the sides.[1]

Part of the machinery which Fulton had ordered from Boulton & Watt arrived in New York in 1805, and the residue in 1806; and it lay in store until Fulton returned and got his craft in readiness to receive it in 1807.

Livingston returned to New York whilst the boat was in process of construction, and in the spring of 1807 the vessel "was launched from the ship-yard of Charles Brown, on the East River,"[2] and called the *Clermont* — after the name of the private residence of Mr. Livingston on the Hudson River, above Hyde Park. In August, Mr. Fulton made his first trip to Albany and back, at an average speed of about five miles an hour. His water-wheels were hung upon the ends of the shaft, without anything beyond the gunwales of the boat to support them; and they were not covered with a wheel-house or guards. The speed of the boat answered the requirements of the previous acts of the Legislature of New York, which at its next session passed another act, extending to Livingston & Fulton, in addition to the former grant, five years for each boat they should thereafter build, not to exceed in any case the term of thirty years; and by the same act

1 The *Phœnix* was completed but a few days after Fulton's boat; but by Livingston & Fulton's exclusive right was driven from the navigation of the Hudson, and Robert L. Stevens adopted the bold plan of taking her, by sea and the capes of the Delaware, around to Philadelphia; which was safely done, in the face of a severe storm, in the month of June, 1808. Young Stevens, then, acquired the honor of making the first ocean voyage in a steamboat.

2 *Life of Fulton*, p. 167.

made it a penal offense for any one to interfere with the monopoly or exclusive rights granted to these parties.

The *Clermont* immediately commenced to run as a passenger boat between New York and Albany; and in the mean time, to meet the demands for freight and public travel, they proceeded to build several other boats, which they put upon the river, and for some years held the sole and exclusive enjoyment of its waters. This prosperous state of affairs, however, was destined to be of no long continuance with them. The State of New Jersey did not recognize the validity of the New York statutes, at least so far as its own waters of the Hudson were concerned, and by way of retaliation it granted similar rights to its own citizens; and excluded all steamboats, running under the authority of New York, from coming within her jurisdiction.

This placed the matter in the category, that the New York steamers could not cross to the Jersey shore, nor the Jersey steamers to the city of New York. This aspect of the case began to open the eyes of the people of New York to the nature of the monopoly which had been granted to Livingston & Fulton, and a reaction in public sentiment on the subject commenced. Others, moreover, were desirous of placing boats upon the Hudson and sharing in the profits of the business; while the commercial interests of New York city and the surrounding country demanded the free navigation of the Hudson and adjacent waters of the Sound and Bay of New York, to be flung open to unrestricted intercourse, to all such as chose to use them. Thus the validity of the grant to Livingston & Fulton was questioned, denying the power of the legislature to make it; and relying upon the opinions of eminent counsel to that effect, a company was formed in Albany, in 1810, who put another line of steamers on the river in opposition to the previous grants. This brought the matter to a crisis. Livingston & Fulton filed their bill in Chancery, for a perpetual injunction against the Albany Company, before Chancellor Lansing. The prayer of the petitioners was denied, on the ground that the State grants were invalid, "being repugnant to the Constitution of the United States and against common right." This decree, however, was reversed by the Court of Errors of the State of New York, on the ground that the State Legislature possessed a concurrent power with the General Government, but subordinate to it, in case any actual collision between the two powers should arise. But the Court denied that "any interference had been shown (by the Albany Company) between the State laws and the constitutional powers of Congress to regulate commerce." Hence, on this mere subterfuge, they set aside the decision of the Chancellor; but at the same time advanced the opinion, "that a patent right, granted by Congress, in case of a conflict, would prevail against the State grants;" as "the laws of Congress are paramount and must prevail."

This intimation alarmed Livingston & Fulton, for neither of them claimed or pretended to any patent right in their boats, or to any part of the machinery; nor did they claim any "coasting license under the laws of the United States."[1] In this dilemma,

[1] *New York Review*, vol. iv. p. 151.

application was immediately made to Congress, in the name of Fulton, for a patent for paddle-wheels and other parts of the machinery, supposing if he could secure these by patent, that no one else could run boats against him, as they were necessary in his view to success; and that a patent of this machinery would substantially give the exclusive navigation to him and Livingston, not only of the Hudson, but elsewhere within the waters of the United States. His application was allowed, and a patent was granted to Fulton under date of February 9, 1811, more than twenty years from Read's experiment with paddle-wheels at Danvers, and just twenty years into a day after he filed his petition for a patent for them in Congress.[1] Fortified in their position, as they believed, by the above patents, Livingston & Fulton now proceeded with their plans with renewed confidence; constructed new boats; and in the mean time brought the Albany Company to terms, by allowing them the waters of Lake Champlain, "as their domain."[2] There now appeared to be nothing in the way of a vast fortune before them, as their returns and profits were great, and the advantages they had secured gave every promise of their being still greater; indeed, no one attempted to estimate the value of their business in prospect. And they were the more fortified in their position by obtaining a still further act from the Legislature of New York, imposing additional penalties for any invasion of their rights, and depriving the

[1] Livingston the next year, June 13, 1812, took out a patent in his name also, for propelling boats with paddles and chain-wheels, to give them additional security in their monopoly. See *List of Patents*, p. 174.

[2] *New York Review*, vol. iv. p. 152.

Court of Chancery of all judicial discretion as to the granting of any injunction against them.[1]

This high-toned and arbitrary exercise of legislative power actually placed the matter without the pale of the courts of justice, and beyond the reach of law; and for a time all opposition seemed to be crushed and put to its final rest. But the citizens of New Jersey were not content to have their boats forfeited, as the last New York laws provided, and insisted upon running them from their own shores across the Hudson to the city of New York. They claimed a common interest in the waters, at least, so far as their own territory was bounded upon them, and they refused to pay any respect, or give any heed to the New York Statutes; that they were a free people, and would never consent to pay tribute to Livingston & Fulton. Colonel Aaron Ogden was then Governor of the State of New Jersey; and as a pacific mode of disposing of the matter, he petitioned the legislature of the State of New York to remove the restriction which had been imposed upon their courts, which prevented an approach to the ordinary tribunals of justice for redress, and demanded the privilege of placing a steamer, for public accommodation and the preservation of his own property, upon an ancient ferry he owned, between Elizabethtown Point and the city of New York.

William Duer,[2] whose pen afterwards so effectually exposed the character of this monopoly, and the means used by Livingston & Fulton to obtain it,[3] was a mem-

1 *New York Review*, vol. iv. p. 152.

2 Afterwards President of Columbia College, N. Y.

3 See Duer's first and second letters to Cadwallader D. Colden, 1817.

ber of the committee to whom the memorial of Colonel Ogden was referred. The committee reported in substance, that after the expiration of Fitch's patent, "the right to use the waters of the Hudson became common to all the citizens of the United States;" that it was questionable, whether a State had the power to pass any law interfering with the power of Congress "to regulate commerce between the several States;" and they declared the act of 1811, "to be unjust and violent in its operation," fraught with high and unusual penalties, and closing the door of justice "against any one who might be desirous of bringing his rights to a legal test." And they recommended the passage of an act "to permit the questions left open by the Court of Errors (the constitutional questions) to be judicially examined."

A bill was introduced to that effect and passed the House, but was denied in the Senate. This once more alarmed Livingston & Fulton, and they offered favorable terms of compromise to Colonel Ogden, which he accepted. He consequently stepped down from the high patriotic position he had taken, submitted to the bribe held up before him, and, to use the language of Mr. Duer, "consented to navigate his boat upon his 'ancient and accustomed ferry,' under the banner of the monopoly." [1]

The above adjustment of the controversy between these immediate parties, in no way settled the question in the public mind; and Connecticut, following New Jersey, passed retaliatory laws, prohibiting steamers running under the New York monopoly from navigat-

[1] See Duer's first and second letters to Cadwallader D. Colden, 1817.

ing the waters of that State. These three States had now actually become parties in the controversy. The embarrassments resulting from this legislative warfare were severely felt; and in fact the navigable waters of all these States were to a considerable extent restricted in their accustomed use ; and all who had not a direct interest in the controversy, agreed that it was an unnatural state of things, and that a remedy must be applied in some form to correct the evil.

Thomas Gibbons, who had been an efficient lawyer, but retired from practice, and residing at Elizabethtown, N. J., owned a ferry (by the side of Ogden's) from that place to the city of New York. Without asking any questions he put two steamboats upon his ferry, and determined to test the validity of the New York Statutes. He was a man of eminent legal attainments, boldness, great wealth, and in every respect a formidable contestant for Livingston & Fulton to deal with ; above price or merely selfish motives. As he entered upon the prosecution of his purpose he found Colonel Ogden an active opponent. Ogden now applied to the Chancellor of New York, who felt bound by the laws of his own State, and the former decision of the Court of Errors ; and he allowed a perpetual injunction against Gibbons, on the ground that "no collision was presented in the case between the acts of Congress and the acts of this State ;" which decision was confirmed by a second decision of the Court of Errors.

From this opinion Gibbons at once appealed to the Supreme Court of the United States. This court reversed the decision of the Court of Errors, on the ground that the Statutes of New York, granting the exclusive right to Livingston & Fulton, were repugnant to the powers the Constitution of the United States had vested in Congress to regulate commerce; and that Gibbons having a coasting license under the General Government, "a case of collision was declared to have arisen." This decision, from which there was no appeal, broke down the monopoly and flung open the Hudson and adjacent waters to fair competition, and the unrestricted intercourse of trade, navigation, and commerce upon them. The immediate result was, that steamers of every description, suited to the capacity and purposes of all who choose to engage in building them, were at once put upon the Hudson and the coast, and began rapidly to extend to the great lakes and rivers throughout the Union. And the exclusive grants to Livingston & Fulton — which the legislature of New York had made with a commendable purpose, no doubt, to encourage these enterprising men, but by a mistaken sense of public rights and duty — fell to the ground. These grants no longer stood as sentinels to guard the avenues of trade and travel, but under the wise provisions of our Federal Constitution, and the just demands of a free and enlightened public sentiment, were virtually obliterated from the records of the State of New York.

The above decision of the United States Court gave vast additional importance to navigation by steam; it opened the whole country to its use, growth, and expansion; and the beneficial results that have followed this settlement of the controversy by the national judiciary are beyond estimate. It in fact gave to steam navigation in America an impetus — for as yet it had scarcely been introduced into any other country — which no human power could limit. In a very few years, not only the Hudson, but the St. Lawrence, the Mississippi, the Ohio, and the Great Lakes, were, if I am allowed the expression, alive with boats of all sizes propelled by steam, passing into and through the hitherto inaccessible territories of the Union, and peopling them with millions of inhabitants from the old States, and from foreign immigration. Such was the effect of American enterprise and genius, when left to their own free action ; and such was the result of that small beginning, in our own land, and by our own native citizens, which prepared the way for this wonderful revolution.

No. 12

CHAPTER XVI.

THAT it may more fully appear how much Read contributed to the development of this great work, we will now proceed to show by comparison, the close analogy that existed between his inventions and combinations, which he applied to his boat, and the machinery which Fulton applied to his two first boats upon the Hudson, — the *Clermont* and the *Car of Neptune*. By this comparison, the fact that Fulton adopted the machinery of Read, not only in its kind, but in its combination, will become self-evident. And the idea that Read's inventions and labors were appropriated by Livingston & Fulton, in the construction of their first boats, will be difficult to overcome; for as already seen, they or either of them did not claim to be the inventors of any part of the machinery they used.

By recurrence to Read's petitions to Congress, and his patent, specifications, and drawings, it is seen that he applied the paddle-wheel as the best mode of propulsion.[1]

That his boiler dispensed with the brick work, was rendered light and portable, and placed in the bottom of the boat.

That his cylinder was fixed at such distance above

[1] See Fig. No. 12 on opposite page; also Plate 3, Fig. 5, p. 102, *ante*.

the boiler as to admit the axis of the float wheels [1] to turn freely, and be raised or lowered at pleasure.

That the floats of the wheels were to be in proportion to the size of the boat, and the velocity with which it is to be moved.

That the axis of the wheels was to be turned by pinions or cranks, as may be found best.

That in lieu of the working-beam, he invented the cross-head, or working frame, running in grooves, either horizontally or vertically, thus dispensing with the working-beam.

That he also dispensed with the parallel motion as invented by Watt.

That he produced the continuous rotary motion to turn the float-wheels, by means of two racks acting alternately, with flexible teeth, or by cranks, and showed that a fly-wheel would not be necessary, as the float-wheels themselves would serve as a substitute, and keep up the motion beyond the dead points.

That he proposed the double-acting cylinder in which the piston was moved by high steam, or by condensation either, as might be found best, but preferred the high steam.

That he dispensed with the cold-water cistern of Watt, and supplied the boiler by injecting water through a pipe passing through the bottom of the vessel or up the side.

That his cross-head is attached to the end of his piston-rod, and is moved by it. And that the cross-head is, moreover, connected with the two racks, or two

[1] Paddle-wheels, float-wheels, side-wheels, and sometimes wheels, are used synonymously.

No. 13

cranks (as the case may be) by two connecting rods, passing from each end of the cross-head to the shaft or axis of the water-wheels.

That he attached his paddle-wheels to the axles of the racks or cranks, without any fly-wheel; which axles were so constructed as to raise or lower their axis of motion at pleasure, to overcome the difficulty that would arise from sinking the wheels too deep in the water, as the vessel became heavily laden.

The machinery Fulton used is described by Professor Renwick as follows: —

"A far more simple form of the engine, and which is in many respects preferable, is that which is used by Fulton in his steamboats. It will be at once seen by inspection, that in this engine the beam is suppressed, together with the parallel motion. As a substitute for these parts, a cross-head is adapted to the upper extremity of the piston-rod; this works between vertical guides: it is connected to the two cranks by the two connecting rods, and to these is joined in the case before us, the axis of the water-wheels." [1]

"The engine which was used in Fulton's final and successful experiment, and which was constructed from the draughts made by Fulton in France, in 1803, had a marked influence upon the forms of those subsequently constructed for this purpose, both in England and the United States. The cold-water cistern of Watt's engine was dispensed with, and in order to supply its place the diameter of the condenser was doubled; its capacity thus became half that of the cylinder, instead of one eighth, as had before been customary. The water of injection was supplied by a pipe passing through the bottom of the vessel. A parallel motion seems to have been sent out as a part of the engine; but, for reasons which

[1] Renwick's *Treatise on the Steam-engine*, p. 163. See Fig. No. 13.

cannot now be discovered, a cross-head, adapted for another purpose to the piston-rod, was made to work in guides. This cross-head was added for the purpose of bearing two connecting rods, or straps, by which two working-beams, as it were, suspended."[1]

"In Fulton's first boat the paddles were attached to the axles of the cranks, and the latter also bore spur-wheels which drove pinions; upon the axles of the pinions was placed a heavy fly-wheel. The paddle-wheels themselves act as regulators, and fly-wheels are, in consequence, no longer to be seen in American steamboats."[2]

"The object proposed by Fulton, in the mode we have described, of connecting his water-wheels with his engine, was unquestionably that of enabling him to change their diameter, and to raise and lower their axis of motion, until he should by experiment ascertain the size and position most advantageous in practice. In conformity with this view of the subject, it is known that the position of the axis was more than once changed; and it is believed that the diameter of the wheel was also altered before the first steamboat was considered by him completed. In the *Car of Neptune*, the second boat Fulton built, he made very important changes in his engine. The piston-rod was still directed by a cross-head, moving in guides, but the working-beams were suppressed altogether, and two cranks, adapted to two separate axles, were attached directly to the cross-heads by connecting rods. A fly-wheel was still used, driven by wheels and pinions, and in the slow rate of motion, to which he restricted himself, was found of great value. This form of engine is still much used, with the omission, however, of the fly-wheel."[3]

1 See *Essay on the Steamboats of the United States*, by James Renwick, LL. D., in Woolhouse's edition of Tredgold *On the Steam-engine*, Appendix, p. 102.

2 *Ibid.* pp. 102, 103.

3 *Ibid.* p. 103.

"Four miles per hour was the condition to Livingston & Fulton, and Fulton built his first boat with reference to that rate of speed; but by raising the axle and increasing the diameter of the water-wheels, the velocity of the first successful steamboat (the *Clermont*) was carried up to six miles per hour."[1]

"The form of the engine adopted by Stevens differed less from the original form of that of Watt than the form chosen by Fulton. The parallel motion and working-beam were both retained; the connecting-rod was increased somewhat in length, and the axle of the crank produced on both sides in order to form the axle of the paddle-wheels; the enlarged conductor, as a substitute for the cold-water cistern, was also used by him.

"These forms of engines, thus brought into use by Fulton and Stevens, have directed the practice of American engines. The fly-wheel has been laid aside, and the parallel motion has been superseded, even in the engine, with the lever-beam, by a cross-head and slides. Upon the Mississippi and in a few instances in the Atlantic States, horizontal engines have been employed; and the description of engine called high-pressure, in contradistinction to the condensing, is much used in the Western waters."[2]

Mr. Fulton, in his letter to Boulton & Watt, on ordering his machinery, —

"Made inquiries as to the employment of high degrees of heat in small engines, and the limit to which it might be

[1] Tredgold *On the Steam-engine*, Appendix, p. 103.

[2] *Ibid.* p. 104. "In the steamboats of the Ohio and Mississippi high-pressure engines are now in most general use. The boilers are usually cylindrical, with internal flues, and the favorite position of the cylinder is horizontal." —*Renwick*, p. 291.

"The engine Fulton put into the *Savannah*, the first boat he built for ocean navigation, was a horizontal engine." —*Ibid.*

carried, in order to render them light and compact, — for this with his views was necessarily a cardinal point, — and then went on to say, 'The object of my investigation is to find whether it is possible to apply the engine to working boats up our long rivers in America. The only thing that is wanting is to arrange the engine as light and compact as possible,' etc. And in the postscript of his letter, he proposes for Mr. Watt's consideration some schemes of engines suggested by Mr. Livingston. The diameter of the cylinder (made for Fulton) was twenty-four inches with a stroke of four feet, being about nineteen horse-power; — the planning and execution of the subordinate parts, as well as of the connecting and paddle machinery, having been undertaken by Mr. Fulton himself."[1]

The following summary will more directly show the close analogy between the machinery invented and combined by Read, and that used by Fulton as above described.

Read applied paddle-wheels at the sides of his boat, suspended to a shaft or axle passing across the gunwales of the boat; and had no wheel-house.	Fulton used the same in the same way; and had no wheel-house.
Read proposed to turn the axle of his wheels by racks and pinions or by cranks, as might be found best; — he used cranks in his experimental boat.	Fulton used cranks to turn his water-wheels, with a spur-wheel and pinion to move his fly-wheel.
Read constructed his boat so as to raise or lower his water-wheels at pleasure.	Fulton constructed his boat so as to raise and lower the wheels; which he did more than once in his first experiment.
Read proportioned the diameter of his water-wheels and size of his floats to the size and proposed velocity of the boat.	Fulton altered the diameter of his water-wheels until he arrived at the same thing, — a proper proportion of the wheels to the boat.

[1] *Life of Watt*, pp. 333, 334.

Read so changed the engine of Watt as to make it light and portable for river navigation, dispensing with the brick work and other heavy and bulky parts of Watt's engine.

Fulton in his order to Boulton & Watt, wished only certain parts of the common engine; and explained to them that he wanted the unusual machinery he had ordered to make his engine as light and compact as possible, for river navigation in America.

Read's boiler was very compact, multi-tubular, and placed in the bottom of the boat.

Fulton's boiler was compact, with two flues passing through the water, and placed in the bottom of the boat.

Read dispensed with the cold-water cistern of Watt, and fed his boiler by a pipe passing up from the water below the boat; he proposed to dispense with the condenser and ejection-pipe, or not, as might be desired in boats.

Fulton dispensed with the cold-water cistern of Watt, and supplied his boiler and condenser from the water below the boat; he used a condenser with his injection-pipe passing up through the bottom of the vessel.

Read dispensed with the working-beam, and invented the cross-head, or working frame, as a substitute; to be run in guides, either vertically or horizontally.

Fulton dispensed with the working-beam in the building of his second boat, the *Car of Neptune;* and used the cross-head in both boats, with guides in a vertical position.

Read dispensed with the parallel motion as invented by Watt.

Fulton dispensed with the same.

Read used the double-acting cylinder of Watt.

Fulton used the same.

Read did not use the fly-wheel, but claimed that the water-wheels themselves would carry the motion beyond the dead points, and serve the same purpose, making a fly-wheel unnecessary.

Fulton at first used a fly-wheel for his slow motion; but as the velocity of motion was increased, and the speed of his boats became more rapid, fly-wheels were found to be unnecessary, and went out of use.

It is believed that the above comparison is correct; if such be the case, it shows that the machinery which Fulton used was substantially the same as that invented by Read in 1789, for the same purpose to which Fulton applied it in 1807. It is not claimed that Fulton did or did not know that Read was the author of it; but it is claimed that he knew no part of it was of his own invention. But this is clear: that it was a combination of machinery invented and put in successful operation under the labors of these two men, unlike anything of the kind which had before or elsewhere been effected. It was adapted to the purpose for which it was designed, and by its invention and skillful application, gave success to steam navigation.

In relation to one part of the above machinery, the paddle-wheels, which Fulton patented in 1811, the following extract from a letter from Judge Read to Hon. Timothy Pickering, of the date of January 27, 1817, will be read with interest. After speaking of the original draught of certain parts of his steam-engine, copied by Mr. Gray, he proceeds in his letter to say: [1] —

"On the same sheet of paper is a drawing, and in the same manuscript a description of a steamboat, constructed with paddle-wheels, in the same manner they are now used. This drawing of the boat was taken about the same time from one which I built and rowed myself across Porter's River, in Danvers, in the year 1789, in presence of Dr. Prince, of Salem. I have good reason to believe that this was the first boat ever constructed with paddle-wheels, with an avowed intention of propelling it by steam.

"On the 8th of February, 1790, about two months before the passing of the act to 'Promote the Progress of the Useful Arts', I presented a petition to Congress for a patent for the above and other inventions, as will appear by the

[1] It will be recollected that Mr. Pickering had been Secretary of State, and *ex-officio* Commissioner of Patents.

Journals of the House, and by my petition (if kept on file), a copy of which I have preserved. Some months after presenting this petition, I unluckily discovered, by looking into some of the first volumes of the 'Philosophical Transactions,' that an experiment had been made on board a French frigate, with a view to ascertain the comparative utility of wheels and oars in a calm.

"Unacquainted with the spirit of the law, and not knowing that a new application was deemed a new invention, I took out a patent on a new petition for a steamboat, in the year 1791, to be propelled through the water by chain-wheels, — scrupulously avoiding the simple wheel, — which answered my purpose perfectly well, supposing I should not be entitled to a patent for it, in consequence of its having been applied in another way on board a frigate. On the above statement of facts, which I can verify, *Query*, whether a patent for the above inventions, should I take one out, would be valid and of any use to me?

"The law requires that the invention should not be known or used before the application. The engine and boat with paddle-wheels, were not known and used at the time I first applied for a patent; but my application was before the passage of the above act. Will my application to Congress before the passage of the act, be considered in law equivalent to an application to the Secretary of State?

"The above questions are interesting to me, and I should like to have your opinion upon them when you are at leisure, if you will take the trouble to give it. Another question on which I should like to have your opinion, is, whether the experiment made on the boat, constructed in the manner above mentioned, and with the avowed design of propelling it by steam, will any way invalidate Mr. Fulton's patent, so far as it includes the use of paddle-wheels of the same construction I invented and used many years before he applied for a patent?"

CHAPTER XVII.

It is proper here to make the inquiry, how Fulton came by this unique system of machinery? Did he get it from Fitch, or Symington, or Bell, who are the only persons, hitherto, for whom any pretensions of that sort appear to have been made?

Aaron Vail, American Consul at L'Orient in France, had made a contract with Fitch and his company, "with a view to obtain patents in France and other parts of Europe."[1] In pursuance of this contract Fitch went to France in 1793, but succeeded in doing nothing; and soon left on account of the political agitations in France, which superseded all business operations.[2] On leaving, Fitch deposited his papers with Vail, who lent them to Fulton for his inspection, as Mr. Vail was heard to remark;[3] but there is no evidence direct from Vail himself on the subject. It is mere hearsay evidence, yet there is no object or disposition to question its correctness. The point of inquiry is, did Fulton use any part or parcel of Fitch's inventions in his boat? To this inquiry the unqualified answer is, that he did not. Did he use Fitch's oars or paddles? Certainly not. Did he use his pipe-boiler? Certainly not. Did he use his ponderous brick-work boiler, that occupied with his other machinery two thirds of his

[1] *Life of Fitch*, p. 320. [2] Duer's second letter to Colden.
[3] *Life of Fitch*, pp. 387, 388.

boat? Certainly not. Did he apply his crank to move twelve oars, six up and six down, or four broad paddles in the stern of his boat? Certainly not. Did he use the pump and trunk, which Fitch at length chose to patent as a mode of propulsion in addition to his oars and paddles? Certainly not. Did he use the trunk Fitch patented, for forcing air out at the stern of his boat, in lieu of water, as a mode of propulsion? Certainly not. Did he use Fitch's leaky wooden caps to his cylinders, or Voight's pipe-con denser? Certainly not. Did he use Hall's, or Thornton's condenser, or Voight's forcing-pump, tried and flung aside by Fitch? Certainly not. Did he use the cold-water tub or cistern in which Fitch placed his condenser? Certainly not. What of Fitch's machinery, then, did he use?

Take the parts above enumerated from any one of the boats Fitch built, and there would be nothing left of his machinery except the double-acting cylinder, which was Watt's invention, and which all alike adopted and used. Hence it is clear that Fulton used no part of Fitch's machinery; and if he in fact had access to Fitch's plans and drawings in the hands of Vail, it proves nothing, except the fact that he did not adopt and use any part of them, but rejected them *in toto*. In short, the whole system of machinery employed by Fulton was different from that of Fitch; and most of it necessarily different, to meet a different plan of construction and propulsion.

It is claimed by English authors, as before seen, that Fulton examined Symington's boat on the Forth and Clyde Canal in 1804, the *Charlotte Dundas*, and that he took drawings of the machinery;[1] hence they infer, that Symington was the man who supplied Fulton with the necessary information for building a steam-boat. Symington was at work upon the above boat three years; he began it in 1801, and commenced to run it upon the canal in 1803, for the purpose of towing ordinary canal boats. But he did not succeed in drawing the boats more than two and a half miles an hour,[2] a speed about the same as that usually performed by horses, and at a much dearer rate. This did not meet the expectation of Symington, and his patron, Lord Dundas, who was a large stockholder in the canal, and the project was flung aside and abandoned. The washing of the banks of the canal was also a difficulty in the way of this mode of towing.[3]

Just as in the case of Fitch, if he took drawings of Symington's boat, it proves nothing. It is not whether he took sketches, but whether he actually used the machinery of Symington's boat. This, neither Mr. Woodcroft, Woolhouse, Lardner, or any one else, has ever ventured to assert. If these gentlemen had made a comparison between the several parts of Symington's machinery and the machinery of Fulton, and found that the làtter was substantially identical with the former, it then would have showed something, and made a very different case of it. But there was one of the best reasons in the world for not doing this, — and the reason was, that in point of fact the machinery of the two did not bear the slightest resem-

[1] Woodcroft's *History of Early Steam Navigation*, pp. 64, 65.

[2] *Life of Fulton*, p. 128.

[3] *Review of the Steam-Engine*, by Dio Lardner. See *New York Review*, vol. v. pp. 98, 99.

blance; and by comparing it, it would prove at once that Fulton adopted and used no part of Symington's.

The "Encyclopædia Britannica," in speaking of the introduction of steam navigation, attributes the whole thing to Symington. In its great purpose of presenting to the world an impartial and exact account of everything, it remarks on this subject:[1] —

"Leaving undescribed some abortive attempts of Rumsey and Fitch in America, which were attended with no practical results, we pass on to the first really successful attempts at steam navigation, which were made in 1788, by a Scotch gentleman, Patrick Miller, of Dalswinton. After trying men and horses to turn the paddle-wheels, he resolved to try the steam-engine to do the work. He went to Edinburgh where he saw Symington, and engaged him to procure an engine; which was built in Edinburgh under Symington's directions, sent to Dalswinton, and put together. The engine, in a strong oaken frame, was placed on one side of a twin, or double pleasure-boat, and the boiler was placed on the other side, and the paddle-wheel in the middle. It was a perfect success," etc.

It then speaks of Symington's boat, which he built for Miller on the canal, and adds: —

"Although these experiments were thus practically successful, and their value well understood and appreciated, we find that Mr. Miller's boat was soon after dismantled and laid up, and nothing further was at that time attempted; that Symington's machinery was not at this time equal to the task of propelling a boat; but the practicability of steam navigation was settled by Miller;[2] but not until 1801 was

[1] Pages 637, 638.

[2] These experiments of Miller did not compare in importance with the previous experiments of Fitch; — no wonder he should choose to leave Fitch's "abortive attempts," undescribed.

a really practicable steamboat first produced; — the *Charlotte Dundas* may justly be considered the first practical steamboat."[1]

In allusion to Fulton, the "Encyclopædia Britannica" adds: —

"We now arrived at the period when American enterprise stepped in to avail itself of the painful and laborious results of these costly experiments. About a year after Symington's experiments with the *Charlotte Dundas*, Fulton, the American engineer, made a similar, though less successful experiment on the Seine, for the weight of his engine broke his vessel in two, and the whole went to the bottom. In August, 1803, he completed another vessel, with its machinery. This boat was sixty-six feet long and eight feet wide, and moved so slowly that his experiment is described as a failure. He afterwards came to Scotland, and saw Symington's steamboat on the Forth and Clyde Canal; his visit being thus recorded by Symington: 'When engaged in these experiments I was called upon by Mr. Fulton, who told me he was lately from North America, and intended returning thither in a few months.[2] In compliance with his request I caused the engine-fire to be lighted up, put the steamboat in motion, and carried him four miles on the canal and returned in one hour and twenty minutes — at the rate of six miles per hour. He asked my consent to take notes, to which I assented. In consequence, he pulled out a memorandum book, and after putting several pointed questions respecting the general construction and effect of the machine,

1 The *Charlotte Dundas* is described as having "a single paddle-wheel, revolving in a well-hole, near the stern of the vessel."

2 Fulton had then been in Europe over seventeen years, and did not return till December, 1806; and, before the above talk, had tried his experiments in France with success, and ordered his engine for a boat on the Hudson.

which I answered in a most explicit manner, he jotted down particularly everything then described, with his own observations upon the boat during the trip.'

"Fulton having obtained what information he could, returned shortly afterwards to America, and in conjunction with Mr. Livingston, obtained a patent securing to them prospective advantages of steam navigation in America, by what they were pleased to call 'their invention of steamboats.'"

It will be remembered that Fulton went over to England from France in 1804, and when he visited Symington's boat it must have been between that time and December, 1806. And the "Encyclopædia" as well as Symington, both state that it was after Fulton's experiment on the Seine, which was in August, 1803.[1] This shows that Fulton had no draughts and plans from Symington prior to ordering his engine. And it is, moreover, not claimed, that he received any other draughts and plans than what he jotted down on his pocket memorandum, with open hand and pencil, during the short trip of one hour and twenty minutes on the canal. Such are the boasted plans and draughts furnished by Symington to Fulton, and such the grounds of pretension of British standard works, that America is indebted to England for her steamboats.

Indeed, the experiments of Symington were insignificant, when compared with several experiments which had been made in this country before. Fitch

[1] See *ante*, pp. 167, 170. "In August, 1803, he completed another vessel with its machinery, sixty-six feet long, eight feet wide, which moved so slow it is described as a failure. Afterwards he came to Scotland, and saw Symington's steamboat," etc.

had run his boat three months as a passenger boat on the Delaware. Morey had experimented with his boat, — a far better one than Symington's. Livingston had tried his first, and yet neither they nor Symington had hit upon the right sort of machinery.

Professor Renwick, in his "Treatise," says: "A comparison of the draught of Symington's boat, which is still extant, with the boats constructed by Fulton, furnishes conclusive evidence that the latter borrowed no valuable ideas from the former." In an able article, said to be written by the same author, he adds: [1] —

"It is a remarkable fact, which more than any other establishes the value of Fulton's experiment, that this identical form (of his engine) without change or modification of any real importance, is still to be found in the greater part of the steamers of Great Britain (1838), and was seen but a few days since in three of them in the harbor of New York. It is wholly and essentially different from that used by Stanhope, Miller, or Symington, or from that subsequently adopted by Fulton himself. The inference is direct, that the steam navigation of Great Britain was not improved by gradual steps from the earlier imperfect experiments, but adopted, from the first dawn of its success, the plans of Fulton; while he had in no respect imitated those earlier experiments, but modified the original engine of Watt to a form consistent with his own views." [2]

It is not claimed that Symington effected this modification of Watt's engine, which in fact fitted the steam-engine for navigation, and is in reality the substance of the whole controversy. Had he effected this work, his English contemporaries, in their endeavor to attach

[1] See *New York Review*, vol. iii. p. 102. [2] *Ibid.* p. 102.

every possible improvement of the steam-engine to Englishmen, would not have failed to mention it, and give the details of the improvement. And had Boulton & Watt, who built Symington's last engine for him, been aware of any such improvement, they would not have been surprised at the unusual machinery embraced in Fulton's order; which required Fulton's explanation and personal attendance and supervision, in order to construct it; as "a new form of engine was indispensable for the purpose he intended to apply it."[1]

Fulton in his order proposed no alteration in the cylinder, but directed the condenser to be enlarged, the cold-water cistern to be dispensed with, and the water for condensation to be supplied by a vertical pipe through the bottom of the vessel, a cross-head to the piston-rod in lieu of the working-beam and parallel motion, the cross-head to work in guides, and the machinery so constructed as that he might raise or lower the axle of the paddle-wheels at pleasure.[2] All these arrangements were new to Boulton & Watt, and required special plans and directions to construct the machinery. Such surely would not have been the case had Symington ordered and procured the same machinery from them in 1801. From the above circumstance, in the absence of all evidence showing the several parts of Symington's engine, it is safe to conclude, that it did not vary in any essential particular from the ordinary engines of that day; while that used by Fulton was a new thing entirely, the double-acting

[1] *New York Review*, vol. iii. p. 101. [2] *Ibid.*

cylinder of Watt excepted. And the draught of Symington's boat, made by himself, it appears from the above statement of Professor Renwick, "furnishes conclusive evidence" of the fact, that Fulton was in no way indebted to him for his machinery.[1]

The claim that Bell furnished Fulton with plans and drawings in 1806, has been sufficiently answered on a former page. Before the above date, Fulton's machinery had been ordered, built, and sent to New York. And although Bell was the first to construct a successful steamboat in Great Britain, he did not commence it until 1811, and put it in operation in 1812; and it is conceded on all hands, that the boat Bell built — the *Comet*—was copied after Fulton's boats; which mode of construction, without any essential improvement, is still followed in England. If Bell, in the words of Mr. Woolhouse, "sent a description of the method of applying steam in propelling vessels against wind and tide, to all the emperors and crowned heads of Europe, and also to America, which last government put it

1 "Symington's water-wheel is situated in a cavity near the stern, and in the middle of the breadth of the boat, so that it becomes necessary to have two rudders, one on each side, connected together by rods, which are moved by a winch near the head of the boat, so that the person who attends the engine may also steer. The piston is supported in its position by friction wheels, and communicates by means of a joint with a crank connected with a wheel, which gives the water-wheel, by means of its teeth, a motion somewhat slower than its own; the water-wheel serving as a fly-wheel. He had stampers at the head of the boat for the purpose of breaking ice on the canal in winter." For the above description see *Gregory's Mechanicks*, vol. ii. p. 423.

The above drawing of Symington's boat (see No. 14), is given in Dr. Young's *Natural Philosophy*, vol. i. London, 1817. It will be seen from the description and drawing, that there was scarcely a resemblance between Symington's and Fulton's boats.

No. 14

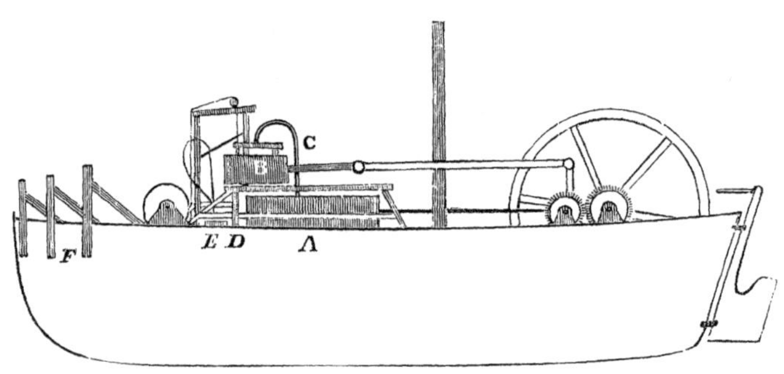

in practice in the year 1806," it is certainly very strange, that no account of the doings of our government has ever been known or published on the subject. It must be concluded that our government was as shy in building steamboats after the plans of Mr. Bell, as were the emperors and crowned heads of Europe themselves, who it seems were not moved by Bell's letters missive. In short, the pretensions in behalf of Bell are fabulous, so far as the invention of Fulton's machinery is concerned; but that he constructed a small boat at Glasgow, at his own risk and expense, after the fashion of Fulton's, which was the first successful boat in England, is not doubted; but it was five years after Fulton built his boat upon the Hudson.

This story about Bell, probably had its origin from the following circumstance; which furnishes no just ground, and in fact no ground whatever, for Mr. Woolhouse to make the claim for him as the inventor of Fulton's machinery: —

"Among the workmen who were sent out from Soho (Boulton & Watt's shop) to put up his (Fulton's) engine, was one of the name of Bell. He speedily returned to Europe, and was, after some years of fruitless endeavors to obtain funds, the first who constructed a successful steamboat in Great Britain. The engine of this vessel (the *Comet*) was an exact copy of that of Fulton, with the exception that the vertical branch of the two suspended beams was suppressed, and the motion of the crank taken off from the end of the beam opposite to that of the piston-rod." [1]

Further comment on this subject is unnecessary.

[1] *New York Review*, vol. iii. p. 102.

CHAPTER XVIII.

If the above view of the subject is correct, neither Fitch, Symington, or Bell, invented any part of Fulton's machinery; and it is not claimed for Fulton that he invented any part of it himself. On this last point it may be well here to make some further examination.

Cadwalader D. Colden, the biographer of Fulton, and his intimate friend and principal counsel, notwithstanding the partiality he manifests for him in every page of his memoir, has the candor to remark: —

"Mr. Fulton had indeed given to Messrs. Boulton & Watt instructions for constructing the first engine which was successfully used in a boat, and had directed its parts to be made so that it might be arranged in a manner, and within a compass suited to his purpose, which no one with a less mechanical genius than himself would have been able to do as accurately as it was done by him; yet he made no pretensions as an inventor with respect to the engine. On the contrary, he has been often heard to declare, that he did not pretend himself to have made any improvement . . . . upon engines which were constructed according to Mr. Watt's principles." [1]

Mr. Colden also says, in a note referring to a "Treatise on propelling Vessels by Steam": —

"Mr. Buchanan (the author of the 'Treatise') very candidly admits that Mr. Fulton is entitled to the merit of hav-

[1] Colden's *Life of Fulton*, p. 120.

ing been the first who contrived the means of usefully applying the power of steam to navigation, which is all that Mr. Fulton ever claimed."[1]

"The claims of Mr. Fulton are defended with great ability by a Mr. Frederick Royou, in a memoir published in the 'Journal des Debats' of the 16th of March, 1816. Mr. Royou presents the true question: 'It is not,' says he, 'concerning an invention, but the means of applying a power already known. Fulton never pretended to be an inventor in regard to steamboats in any other sense.'"[2]

"We now come to Robert Fulton; a man original in many things, but who, as the introducer of the steamboat, merely availed himself of the fruits of the labors and successes of the ingenious men in America and Europe who had toiled before him."[3]

"Fulton began after years wasted by other men in trials by which he profited, and appropriating to himself the principles made manifest by the results of their toils, disappointments, and losses, is now held out to the world as the original inventor of steamboats."[4]

"He (Fulton) was not the original inventor of steamboats. . . . . What was he then? Why, he was the first to gain the prize; he it was who satisfied the law."[5]

"The great and surprising merit of Fulton consisted not so much in absolute originality as in the skill with which he availed himself of all the theoretical knowledge of the day, and applied it to practical purposes."[6]

"That Fulton was the inventor of the present system of steam navigation, as asserted by some American authors, cannot be admitted; nor indeed did he 'invent' any single

1 Colden's *Life of Fulton*, p. 130.
2 *Ibid.* p. 160.
3 *Life of Fitch*, p. 384.
4 *Ibid.* p. 390.
5 *Lives of Eminent Mechanics*, p. 186.
6 *New York Review*, vol. iii. p. 105.

12

improvement in the construction either of the machinery or vessel." [1]

Professor Renwick also states, and so do Woodcroft, Stuart, and Tredgold, that Fulton was not the original inventor of the steamboat or of the machinery he employed in the construction of his boats, but they allow him great and deserved credit for successfully applying the machinery invented by others. Indeed, every person who has written on the subject of steam navigation, who aims to give an impartial view of it, as well as those who were interested for and against the claims of Fulton, allow the same thing. That Fulton, therefore, was not the inventor of the steamboat, nor of the machinery he used, nor indeed of any part of it, may be regarded as a well-settled fact.

Thus seeing that the essential part of the machinery used by Fulton was identical with that invented by Read many years before, and the invention not claimed by Fulton, or traceable to any other source than to Read, is it not reasonable to conclude that he was the author of it, without further inquiry on the subject? But when we turn back to the time he first made his application to Congress, in 1789, and still further see how easy and probable a matter it was for Stevens, Livingston, and Fulton to become acquainted with his inventions and the details of his machinery, it renders it still more certain, that the boat Read invented, was the one adopted by Fulton.

This conclusion is rendered still more certain when it is recollected that Read, after completing his inventions and preparing his draughts and models, as the

[1] *Encyclopædia Britannica*, p. 638.

very first step he took, presented them to the American Academy of Arts and Sciences, for their examination, — which showed not only the confidence he had in his work, but the high and honorable purpose he entertained of submitting it to the scrutiny of the most competent scientific board within his reach before he proceeded further, — moreover, that the committee appointed by the above Academy, which consisted of men of no less distinction than Richard Cranch, Loammi Baldwin, Joseph Willard, and Caleb Gannett, spoke of the originality of his inventions, and the beneficial effects that would be likely to follow from them, and frankly recommended them to the attention of Congress; that he also had a like recommendation from a list of eminent men of Boston and vicinity, among whom were Benjamin Lincoln, James Winthrop, Eliphalet Pearson, and Nathaniel W. Appleton, in which they say "that they were original inventions so far as they know;" and furthermore that he did not in any way attempt to conceal or make a secret of his discoveries.

Now as we place this matter before us in a single point of view, and notice the opinions expressed by the Academy of Arts and Sciences, and by gentlemen of known erudition and science in addition, as to the originality of the inventions of Read, and on that ground, as well as public utility, recommending the subject to the attention of Congress; that his inventions were publicly exhibited in New York; that they were examined by Stevens and fully explained to him; that Stevens, Livingston, and Rosevelt afterwards entered into partnership for the purpose of building a boat, wherein any information possessed by one would, as a matter of course, be communicated to and be possessed by all; that the models, plans, petitions, and specifications of Read were matter of record, and open to public examination before them; that the first boat this company built in New York, and the first experiment tried by Fulton in France, under the direction of Livingston, after he had retired from the company, were alike to be propelled with the chain-wheel, which alone was to be found in Read's patent; that they finally adopted the paddle-wheel, contained in his first petition to Congress, as in his opinion the best mode of propulsion; and, in short, that nearly all the machinery used by Fulton was the same as that invented by Read, — do they not furnish a succession and concurrence of circumstances, but little if any less convincing than direct and positive testimony, to show that these inventions and improvements of Read found their way to Fulton, in Paris, when Livingston "informed him of what had been attempted in America?"[1]

It is, moreover, claimed for Fulton, if he did not invent, that he combined this machinery. A combination of machinery is ever theoretical in the outset, and is a necessary part and parcel of its invention when applied to the purpose originally designed. When mixed with other machinery, to accomplish some other purpose, a new combination may very properly be claimed. But if applied as designed, the invention and combination are one and the same thing; both the result of the same idea.

The machinery invented by Read was applied to

[1] This introduction of Read's inventions into Paris by Livingston will also show how Seguin may have become acquainted with the multi-tubular boiler. *Ante*, pp. 53, 55, *note* 1, and 63.

the very purpose, and in the same way, it was originally intended by him; hence so far as thus applied, it cannot be said that Fulton was the author of its combination. It is doubtless, however, true that when the machinery came from under the hands of the workmen, prepared for practical use, it received a finish that belonged to the artisans to give it; this would have been done as matter of course, whether ordered by Fulton or Read, or any one else, as may be seen in the finish of the cross-head. But this is merely carrying out the principles of the invention, and applying them to practical use. In short, take from Fulton's boat, Watt's double-acting-condensing cylinder, and the machinery Read invented and combined with it, and there would be but little left beside the naked hull. The fact that Fulton used Watt's cylinder, which came into the combination of Read, in his reconstruction of the steam-engine, does not confront but tends to confirm the idea that Fulton applied Read's machinery, as invented and combined by him.

In further support of what has been shown, both in relation to the steamboat and locomotive engine, the following brief account, written by Judge Read himself seventeen years after his letter to Colonel Pickering, before quoted (see page 164), will be read with interest. It is contained in a letter written by him in reply to some inquiries then made of him by the writer on the subject of his inventions in steam, arising from remarks by Dr. Benjamin Lincoln, former Professor in the University of Vermont, which led to the inquiries.

"BELFAST, *August* 22, 1834.

"DEAR SIR: — Fitch was the first who constructed a steamboat in America; Rumsey was the next. Fitch applied paddles, and could not propel his boat more than four miles an hour. Paddles were subsequently tried on a large scale, and found to be inadequate to the purpose. Rumsey at first used a pump, which drew in water at the bow, and forced it out at the stern of the boat. He next tried setting-poles for river navigation, but without success.[1] Believing their failure was occasioned by their ill-constructed boilers and complex machinery, and believing also that steam might be advantageously applied to land carriages, I constructed in the year 1789 a small boiler, which, from its characteristic principles, I denominated a Portable Furnace Boiler. It occupied but little space —was light and strong — and so constructed as to require no other furnace than what itself constituted. It was especially designed for steamboats and steam-carriages, a model of each of which I had constructed the same year.

" The boat was of sufficient size to carry a man and the necessary apparatus to propel it through the water. To the axis, which extended across the gunnel of the boat, were fixed two paddle-wheels, which were constructed on precisely the same principles they now are for steamboats. With this boat, by means of a crank and without a fly-wheel, I rowed myself, soon after it was finished, with great rapidity, across an arm of the sea, which separates Danvers from Beverly. The Rev. Dr. John Prince, of Salem, and several other gentlemen were present, and saw the experiment. Of this fact I have somewhere among my papers Dr. Prince's certificate.

" I spent a considerable part of the winter of 1790 in the city of New York, and exhibited drawings and descriptions of my steamboat, steam-carriage, etc., to President Washington, to whom I had letters of introduction from General Lincoln, grandfather of the Professor. I also showed them to several members of Congress, and, I presume, to upwards

[1] The setting-poles were probably tried first. — ED.

of fifty other gentlemen (some of them distinguished mechanics) in the city of New York, and explained to them the principles of the machinery and of the boiler designed for steamboats and land carriages.

" I boarded at Mrs. Wheaton's, in company with Dr. Cutler and General Rufus Putnam, who were agents of the Ohio Company; and I recollect perfectly well, they introduced General Stevens to me, and I explained to him the principles on which my boat, boilers, etc., were constructed. If I am rightly informed, I presume this must have been the same gentleman who was afterwards largely concerned in steam navigation, and was at first connected with Chancellor Livingston in building a steamboat.

" I first petitioned the Board of Commissioners for a patent for a steamboat with paddle-wheels; but, unfortunately, in looking over some of the first volumes of the " Transactions of the Royal Society," published upwards of a hundred years ago, I discovered that an experiment had been made on board a French frigate, for the purpose of ascertaining the comparative utility of wheels and oars. Supposing at that time, in consequence of this discovery, that I should not be entitled to a patent for a boat with paddle-wheels, I took considerable pains to invent a substitute, which was a rowing machine, constructed on the principle of the chain-pump.

" Having satisfied myself that this would answer a good purpose, and be the best substitute I could think of for the simple paddle-wheel, which I had successfully tried, I withdrew my first petition to the Board, and took out a patent for my new mode of rowing boats, and for a Portable Furnace Boiler, which required no other furnace than what itself constituted. It was constructed internally with tubes, on the same principle, and nearly of the same form, with those now used for locomotive engines.

"I was too early in my steam projects. The country was then poor; and I have derived neither honor nor profit from the time and money expended on them. But it is gratifying to know that the simple machinery which forty-five years ago (without any knowledge of its having ever been used for that purpose) I selected as the most eligible for propelling boats through water, has been since that time successfully used in every quarter of the globe for that purpose. I was, however, still more gratified last spring, in viewing a locomotive engine, capable of moving a mile in two minutes, put in operation by steam generated in a portable boiler, constructed essentially on the same principle with one which I invented for that and other purposes about forty-six years ago, and for which I obtained a patent the first day that any patent was ever issued by authority of the United States.

"I have a distinct recollection, when my petition to Congress was read in Congress Hall by the Clerk of the House of Representatives, that when he came to that part which related to the application of steam to land carriages, a general smile was excited among the members, and the idea was considered there and at Salem, where I had a model of a steam-carriage constructed, as perfectly visionary.[1]

"Yours truly,

"N. READ."

[1] The article relating to the French frigate above referred to by Judge Read, has been found in vol. vi. of the *Philosophical Transactions of the Royal Society*, extending from 1713 to 1723 inclusive, on page 545 of the condensed work; old vol. xxxi. anno 1721.

The article is headed "A Method for rowing Men-of-war in a Calm. By M. Du Quet. No. 369, p. 239."

It says, "To perfect the art of navigation, two things seem principally wanting, namely, an easy method of finding the longitude at sea, and a way to give a vessel its course in a calm. I flatter myself I have found the last, and hope to make it appear by reason and experiment that a man-of-war may make a league an hour in a calm, by means of revolving oars, which are easily applied to the sides of the ship, without occasioning any incumbrance."

The article proceeds to speak of experiments, but of nothing beyond, to test the comparative merits of common oars and revolving oars, which last, from the description of them, were constructed by attaching arms, with floats upon the ends of them, three feet apart, to a shaft passing across the boat. It also speaks of the capstan and of relays of men to work the revolving oars, and reckons the moving force in proportion to the number of men: and in time of battle could make up to board an enemy in a calm or to haul off, as desired. That's all there is of the article.

CHAPTER XIX.

In anticipation of the inquiry which will very naturally be made, why these facts have not before been collected and presented to the public in a published form, the following brief correspondence and the considerations that follow, it is believed, will satisfactorily show. In a communication of the date of February 25th, 1840, in reply to an intimation to him by a friend that such a publication should be made, Judge Read makes the following brief answer: —

"It is my wish and intention, if my life and health be spared, to collect together and arrange the evidence I have in relation to my improvements and inventions in steam-power, and leave it to posterity, or to some other person than myself, to publish to the world."

The following letter, in allusion to the same subject, was addressed to him by Rev. J. W. Hanson of Danvers, Mass.: —

"Danvers, *June* 1, 1847.

"Hon. Nathan Read: —

"Dear Sir, — I am engaged in writing a History of Danvers, and I wish to give therein a short biographical notice of yourself. Will you favor me with a sketch, so far as you may judge proper? Will you (should you accede to my request) relate particularly the discoveries in steam-power by yourself, giving the dates and localities and other leading facts?

"By complying with my desires as soon as other engagements will permit, you will oblige

"Yours truly,

"J. W. HANSON.

"P. S. — Please address

"REV. J. W. HANSON,

"*Danvers New Mills, Mass.*"

"BELFAST, *June* 6, 1847.

"REV. J. W. HANSON: —

"DEAR SIR, — Your interesting letter of the 1st inst. was duly received, but I have not had leisure as yet to comply with your request. Hope, however, it will not be long before I shall be able to send you a copy of some authentic documents relative to my improvements in the steam-engine, and my contemplated application of it to boats, land carriages, and other useful purposes.

"Should my health continue, I will also give you a brief sketch of my life.

"Respectfully yours,

"NATHAN READ."

Judge Read, at the date of the above letter to Rev. Mr. Hanson, was near the close of the eighty-eighth year of his age; yet he commenced a brief autobiography, agreeable to the above engagement, and proceeded so far as to prepare a synopsis of some of the leading incidents of his life; but before he had carried his purpose beyond a mere memorandum, evidently designed as the basis of an autobiography, he was attacked with a lung-fever, which he did not survive.

At his advanced age, an undertaking so arduous must have been felt by him as a task, and, however desirable, he seems to have made but little progress during the brief space of time that remained for him;

and, indeed, his papers, without any particular arrangement, were left "to posterity, or to some other person than himself, to publish to the world," evidently against the purpose he formed when too late, but in accordance with his intention as expressed in his letter to his friend in 1840. It is much to be regretted that his life and health should not have been spared sufficiently long, after he formed his new purpose, to have carried it out, and thus have given to the world, from under his own hand, a more satisfactory and intelligent account of his labors than can now be done.

In addition to the above facts, there are many considerations that may be brought to view to account for his delay in presenting these inventions to the public. At the time of effecting these improvements he labored under the weight of a strong popular prejudice against their utility, and possessed no adequate means himself to carry his inventions into practical effect, and was forced to suspend his prosecution of the subject, under the hope that a more enlightened public sentiment, and circumstances more favorable to his means of progress, would come to his aid. In this shape the matter rested through many years of discouragement, until he became engaged in other pursuits; and others, in the mean time, stepped in to reap the benefit of his improvements, and enjoy the fame of his inventions.

About the time Fulton put his boat upon the Hudson (which indeed was the same year), he retired to his farm in Belfast, which, for the remainder of his life, occupied a great share of his attention. It gave him but little opportunity to enter into a controversial warfare in relation to his priority, and the legal privileges secured to him by patent had already expired by lapse of time. He was, moreover, a man of peace, and naturally disinclined to thrust himself before the public in a controversy which promised to him no other result than the gratification of personal ambition or pride.

Under such circumstances, it is in no way surprising that the matter should be suffered to pass along until he arrived at the conclusion to arrange his evidence, and leave it to posterity to present to the world. In the mean time his own personal friends and acquaintances, though acquainted with the general facts in relation to his inventions, yet felt that so long as he lived the whole matter was under his own control, and that it would be out of place to disturb in any way the free action and purpose of his own mind on the subject.

Since his decease the subject has rested until these few unpretending pages have been written, in the hope and purpose that they would be instrumental in preserving the history of the important part he took in the reconstruction of the steam-engine, and its successful preparation for navigation and land transport.

As we contemplate the vast results that have followed the application of steam-power to these purposes, it can do no less than inspire us with a veneration for the men who were the genuine contrivers, as well as constructors, of the work — not for any one who may be a relative, friend, or favorite, but for all who contributed their time, talents, or fortune to it, in proportion to their respective merits. How sublime is the thought that it is they who have created a power and ability in our race to attain to a seemingly higher destiny on earth than before had been allotted to it! It is they, too, who have done so much to extend the arts and sciences, and make them more and more subservient to our use and benefit — a matter that has distinguished the age in which we live.

If Judge Read did not succeed in securing the opportunity of applying his inventions to practice, it is believed, nevertheless, that no one did more than he towards the invention of the successful steamboat and locomotive. As we look back upon the little boat he experimented with at Danvers, just large enough to carry a man, we see that it contained the elements of a successful growth and development; and we have seen but a short time since, a steamer lying in the harbor of New York,[1] of sufficient size and capacity to carry an army of ten thousand men with their equipage, having the same paddle-wheels, the same multi-tubular boilers, and the same type of machinery throughout (save the screw propellers attached as a collateral force) that were invented and combined in the model boat and model engine of Read more than seventy years ago.

Moreover, the present locomotives, in the wonderful exhibition of their power and utility throughout every civilized land, are driven by his multi-tubular boiler and high-pressure engine, which alone give to them their life, availability, and marvelous power, under their present improved state; and although those improvements have been gradually progressing, yet the main features and principles of the machinery remain unchanged.

From the invention of the steamboat and locomo-

[1] The *Great Eastern*.

tive, the greatest that human genius has ever achieved, we may calculate that still greater results are to follow. What they have already accomplished is familiar to all; and our national pride as well as individual satisfaction, are exultingly felt as we attach these inventions to our own country, and as we behold with wonder how great an influence they together have exerted, not only on the products of industrial labor and the extension of trade and commerce, but on the whole order of society, the advance of civilization, and the spread of Christianity; but the future alone can tell how far this display of ingenuity and mental power will reach.

APPENDIX.

No. 1.

SPECIFICATION AND PATENT OF NAIL MACHINE.

"*The United States of America. To all to whom these Letters-patent shall come :* —

"WHEREAS, Nathan Read, a citizen of the State of Massachusetts in the United States, hath alleged that he has invented a new and useful improvement, to wit, a machine for cutting and heading nails at one operation. . . . . which improvement has not been known or used before his application; has made oath that he does verily believe that he is the true inventor or discoverer of the said improvement; has paid into the Treasury of the United States the sum of thirty dollars, delivered a receipt for the same, and presented a petition to the Secretary of the United States, signifying a desire of obtaining an exclusive property in the said improvement, and praying that a Patent may be granted for that purpose: These are, therefore, to grant according to law, to the said Nathan Read, his heirs, administrators, or assigns, for the term of fourteen years from the thirteenth day of the month of December last past, the full and exclusive right and liberty of working, constructing, using, and vending to others to be used, the said improvement; a description whereof is given in the words of the said Nathan Read himself, in the schedule hereto annexed, and is made a part of these Presents.

"In testimony whereof, I have caused these Letters to be made Patent, and the Seal of the United States to be hereunto affixed. Given under my hand at the city of Philadelphia, this eighth day of January, in the year of our Lord one thousand seven hundred and ninety-eight, and of the independence of the United States of America the twenty-second. JOHN ADAMS.

[L. S.] By the President,

"TIMOTHY PICKERING, *Secretary of State.*"

"*City of Philadelphia, to wit:*

"I do hereby certify, That the foregoing Letters-patent were delivered to me on the sixth day of January, in the year of our Lord one thousand seven hundred and ninety-eight, to be examined; that I have examined the same, and find them conformable to law; and I do hereby return the same to the Secretary of State, within fifteen days from the aforesaid date, to wit, on this eighth day of January, in the year aforesaid.

"CHARLES LEE, *Attorney General.*"

"The schedule referred to in these Letters-patent, and making part of the same, containing a description in the words of this said Nathan Read himself, of an improvement, to wit: a machine for cutting and heading nails at one operation: —

"Specification of a machine for cutting and heading nails at one operation, invented by Nathan Read of Salem, in the County of Essex and Commonwealth of Massachusetts. The principal parts of this machine are as follows, namely: the cutting tool, which vibrates to cut the heads and points; vices that are shut by weights; hammers that are impelled upward by springs to head the nails; a cantor placed under the cutting tool to cant the nails but-end downward; ducts or tubes to receive the nails from the cantor and convey them to the vices, which are inverted; sliding gauges to stop the nails in their descent, gauge them for the head pendent; levers to move back the sliding gauges, and spiral springs to draw them forward, as occasion requires; shedder to disengage the nails from the vice after they are headed; a stage to support the nail plate, and a pair of nippers, weight, and pully to feed the cutting tool; a complex wheel that gives motion to the other parts of the machine; pillars inverted into a bed-piece which connects and sustains the whole. The wheel, being put in motion by water or any other power as steady, first vibrates the cutting tool to the right, where it receives the nail plate obliquely and cuts the nail, which drops upon the cantor and is thrown but-end foremost into the right hand duct, which conveys it to the vice, where it is stopped by the sliding gauge, adjusted for heading, and held till the vice gripes it; then the sliding gauge is drawn back, and the nail is headed by the hammer. The vice then opens, the shedder strikes the nail, and it drops. The wheel having now completed half a revolution, the position of the cutting tool and cantor is reversed, and a second nail is cut and drops upon the cantor, which cants it but-end downwards into the left-hand duct, through which it descends to the vice below, where it is gauged, headed, and shed, in the same manner as the first was; the large end of the second nail being cut from that part of the plate which formed the point of the first. Thus two nails are cut and headed every revolution of the wheel. For a more particular description, I refer to the drawings, with written references and model, deposited in the office of the Secretary of State. NATHAN READ.

"Witnesses, —
WM. PRESCOTT,
D. W. LEWIS."

No. 2.

ROSEVELT'S VOYAGE DOWN THE OHIO AND MISSISSIPPI.

NICHOLAS J. ROSEVELT was the first who built a steamboat on the Western waters. It was called the *New Orleans*, was launched at Pittsburg, Pennsylvania, in 1811, and was of 100 tons burden. This boat left Pittsburg for New Orleans in October of the same year. It had but one wheel, in the stern, and two masts with sails. The voyage down the Ohio and Mississippi was very adventurous, being the first ever undertaken upon those rivers with a steamboat.[1]

Mr. Rosevelt, wife, a d family, the engineer, pilot, six hands, and a few servants, made up the crew. They arrived safely at the rapids at Louisvill in the night of the fourth day, passing over seven hundred miles in seventy hours. The wild settlers on the banks of the river, who had never heard of such an invention, were struck with surprise and terror at the rapid-going strange thing; and when it arrived late at night at Louisville, it is said the puffing of the steam produced general consternation, and the inhabitants rushed from their beds to find out the cause of the strange noise. The boat was detained about three weeks at Louisville in order to pass the rapids, which she did the last week in November. For two days they pursued their solitary voyage down the Ohio in a hot sun, and still smoky air; as the second night came on, and as they sat quietly upon the deck, "they heard a rushing sound and violent splash, and saw large portions of the shore tearing away from the land and falling into the river. The day had been an awful day; so still that you could have heard a pin drop on deck." They spoke little, for every one appeared thunder-struck.

1 For the following graphic sketch, see account of this voyage by Ch. J. Latrobe, in *The Rambler in North America*.

"The next day, the sun rose over the forests the same dim ball of fire, and the air was thick, dull, and oppressive as before. The portentous signs of this terrific natural convulsion continued and increased. The pilot, alarmed and confused, affirmed that he was lost, as he found the channel everywhere altered; and where he had hitherto known deep water, there lay numberless trees, with their roots upturned. The trees were seen waving and nodding on the bank without a wind; but the adventurers had no choice but to continue their route. Towards evening they found themselves at a loss for a place of shelter. They had usually brought to under the shore, but everywhere they saw the high banks disappearing, overwhelming many a flat boat and raft from which the owners had landed and made their escape.

"A large island, in mid-channel, which was selected by the pilot as the better alternative, was sought for in vain, having disappeared entirely. Thus, in doubt and terror, they proceeded hour after hour till dark, when they found a small island, and rounded to, mooring themselves to the foot of it. Here they lay, keeping watch on the deck, during the long autumnal night; listening to the sound of the waters, which roared and gurgled horribly around them, and hearing from time to time the rushing earth slide from the shore, and the commotions as the falling mass of earth and trees was swallowed up by the river.

. . . . "Several times in the course of the night, the shock of the passing earthquake was communicated from the island to the bow of the vessel. It was a long night, but morning dawned, and showed them that they were near the mouth of the Ohio. The shores and the channel were now equally unrecognizable, for everything seemed changed. About noon they reached the small town of New Madrid; the inhabitants were in the greatest distress and consternation; part had fled in terror to the high grounds, others prayed to be taken on board, as the earth was opening in fissures on every side, and their houses hourly falling around them.

"Proceeding hence, they found the Mississippi, at all times a fearful stream, now unusually swollen, turbid, and full of trees; and after many days of great danger, though they felt no more of the earthquake, they reached their destination at Natchez at the close of the first week in January, 1812, to the great astonishment of all; the escape of the boat having been considered an impossibility. At that time you floated for three or four hundred miles on the river without seeing a human habitation.

"Such was the voyage of the first steamer. The natural convulsion, which commenced at the time of her descent, has been but slightly alluded to, but will never be forgotten in the history of the West; and the changes wrought by it throughout the whole alluvial region through which the Ohio and Mississippi pour their waters, were perhaps as remarkable as any on record."

No. 3.

A COMMITTEE appointed by the House of Commons, as late as 1831, to inquire, among other things, into the present state and future prospects of land carriages run on common roads by steam, after examining Messrs. Gurney, Hancock, Farey, Trevithick, Ogle, Summers, Telford, McAdam, and others on the subject as witnesses, reported a summary of the evidence, as follows, as to the progress made in the application of steam-power to land carriages; and the certainty of their success on common roads.

"1. That carriages can be propelled by steam on common roads at an average rate of ten miles an hour.

"2. That at this rate they have conveyed upwards of fourteen passengers.

"3. That their weight, including engine, fuel, water, and attendance, may be under three tons.

"4. That they can ascend and descend hills of considerable inclination with facility and safety.

"5. That they are perfectly safe for passengers.

"6. That they are not (or need not be if properly constructed) nuisances to the public.

"7. That they will become a speedier and cheaper mode of conveyance than carriages drawn by horses.

"8. That they admit of greater width of line, and as the roads are not acted on by the feet of horses, such carriages will cause less wear of roads.

"9. That the tolls on steam-carriages will prevent their use, if permitted to remain unaltered."

They considered the practicability of running steam carriages on common roads to have been fully established, and that it would result in a very important improvement in the means of communication, and be generally adopted, as scientific men should give their attention to the subject.

Mr. Gurney testified before the committee that in 1829 he travelled from London to Bath and back in his steam-carriage, and performed the last eighty-four miles in ten hours, including stoppages, and afterwards they ran as public stages; that they used tubular boilers, the tubes about one inch in diameter; and that he knew of from twenty to forty other carriages being built.

Mr. Ogle stated that his carriage ran from London to Southampton, and at some places went from thirty-two to thirty-five miles an hour; that they went up and down hills, rising one in six, at a speed of twenty-four miles an hour, laden with passengers, both ladies and gentlemen.

Mr. Summers stated that he had travelled up a hill of one in twelve at the rate of sixteen miles an hour with nineteen passengers, and had run four and a half hours in succession at the velocity of thirty miles per hour.

Mr. James Stone testified that he carried thirty-six persons on one carriage; and Mr. Farey gave it as his opinion that steam-carriages would be run at one-third the expense of coaches.

The other witnesses stated similar facts from their own experiments: one ran his steam-carriage twelve months; and all testified that the carriages were entirely practicable, under perfect control, and, with the slightest movement, could be turned or stopped, where horses would be wholly unmanageable.

Colonel Torrens testified as to the great advantages, in his opinion, that steam-carriages on common roads would have upon British agriculture, as it would open the way for all farming classes to send their produce to market with much greater facility and economy; and that it would tend to reclaim many uncultivated tracts of land, and add much to the aggregate of production from the soil; in addition that the effects from the conveyance of goods and passengers, would be, in amount, almost impossible to calculate.

Parliament had, before the above inquiry, in obedience to the will of the laboring classes, imposed a heavy toll upon the running of land-carriages by steam, which amounted, substantially, to a prohibition of them; and the purpose was to procure a repeal of that law. But Parliament refused to grant the repeal; and the result has been, that railroads have become so numerous, that they now do the business, and have to a considerable extent superseded the necessity, of steam on common roads.

No. 4.

The following is that part of petition No. 2, referred to in the letter by Mr. Remsen (see page 151), relating to land carriages and paddle-wheels.

" *To the Secretary of State, the Secretary for the Department of War, and the Attorney General of the United States*, the petition of Nathan Read of Salem in Massachusetts, most respectfully showeth, That he hath discovered a simple method of moving land carriages by the power of steam, and of directing them principally by the same agent. [Your petitioner hath invented an improved method or methods of impelling boats or vessels through the water, and against the current of rapid rivers, by wheels, etc.[1]] Your petitioner prays, etc. NATHAN READ.

" NEW YORK, *April* 23, 1790."

PETITION No. 1. — The part relating to steam is as follows, namely: —

. . . . "Your petitioner hath increased the utility of the steam-engine by improving the common cylinder in such a manner as to render it a cheap and convenient substitute for the cylinder and case, in which the pressure of steam is substituted for that of the atmosphere. The improved steam-cylinder is so constructed as to work up and down, or back and forth in a horizontal position, with equal power, both ends being closed and alternately exhausted of and replenished with steam. Your petitioner hath also improved the most improved boilers by inventing several portable furnace boilers, each of which is so constructed as to constitute of it-

1 Several other modes are here mentioned; but his specification and drawings show that he relied on wheels, and they are omitted. The brackets were made by Mr. Remsen, and referred to in his letter.

self a furnace or furnaces, the heat of which is advantageously applied to the converting of water into steam, and to the increasing of the expansive power of it before it escapes from the boiler; which exposes within a small space a very large evaporating surface, and is regularly fed with hot water from the reservoir, and also prevents the loss of heat that would take place in a furnace that is foreign to the boiler itself; and on these accounts far less fuel will be consumed upon this than upon any other known construction. Your petitioner prays, etc. "NATHAN READ.

"NEW YORK, *April* 14, 1790."

www.ingramcontent.com/pod-product-compliance
Lightning Source LLC
LaVergne TN
LVHW050524100826
845148LV00002B/428

9781425520397